Inside the World of
CLASSICAL MUSIC

For Chantal,
With all best wishes,

[signature]

12/17/19

205 Illuminating Mini-Essays
Miles Hoffman

For EVA and JILLIAN

Also by Miles Hoffman

The NPR Classical Music Companion:

An Essential Guide for Enlightened Listening

(Originally published as The NPR Classical Music Companion:

Terms and Concepts from A to Z)

AUTHOR'S NOTE

In 2011, I began writing and recording a series of radio modules called *A Minute with Miles*. The "Minutes" are produced by South Carolina Public Radio, and they've been broadcast in South Carolina, North Carolina, and a number of other states. This book consists of a selection of the "mini-essays" I've written for *A Minute with Miles*. As I prepared the book I revised many of the essays and added new material.

ACKNOWLEDGMENTS

Thanks first to South Carolina Public Radio for their commitment to *A Minute with Miles*, and for their courage and dedication in keeping classical music on the air. I'm grateful to the production staff at SC Public Radio, and especially to A.T. Shire, who is far more than an Engineering Manager, and whose good sense, good humor, and consistent encouragement have meant a great deal to me. And my thanks to Spartanburg, SC's own J.M. Smith Corporation, underwriters of *A Minute with Miles* from the beginning. My conversations over the years with composer and violist Max Raimi, violinist Alexis Galpérine, and composer David Berry have deepened and sharpened my thoughts about music. Max kindly read a draft of this book and suggested a number of changes that greatly improved the final product. My primary editor, as always, was my wife, Susan, who makes everything better. She has my gratitude and my love.

Inside the World of
CLASSICAL MUSIC

CONTENTS

II. COMPOSERS

III. PERFORMERS AND PERFORMING

IV. INSTRUMENTS

ABOUT THE AUTHOR

INTRODUCTION

I was talking about music some time ago with a friend who makes his living cloning genes, manipulating molecules, and investigating the fundamental pathways of the human immune system. This is a person whose intellectual molecules are clearly very well arranged. But he proceeded to tell me that although he loved classical music, when he listened to it he wasn't able to perceive anything other than his own emotional reactions.

Could it be true? Well, he thought it was. But he was wrong.

What my friend was expressing was merely a symptom of a common affliction, one that crosses all intellectual, social, and economic classes: the Classical Music Insecurity Complex. Immediate therapy was indicated.

There's no question, I pointed out, that he perceives more than just his own reactions—lots more. In every piece he listens to, he perceives changes, both great and small, in tempo, volume, pitch, voice, and instrumentation. He perceives melodies, harmonies and rhythms, and the patterns they create. He perceives, in short, virtually all the musical ingredients that composers manipulate to stimulate emotional effects, which is precisely why he's emotionally affected. His "problem" isn't perception—it's description. And what he doesn't know is the jargon, the technical terms for the ingredients and manipulations.

And why should he? He's a scientist, not a musician. And frankly, it's not even essential that he be aware of the specific musical and technical means by which his reactions are being stimulated. Years ago I was rehearsing a piece for flute, viola, and piano by the composer Seymour Barab. Mr. Barab was attending the rehearsal, and the pianist asked him at one point if it was important to "bring out," or highlight, a certain clever rhythmic pattern. Mr. Barab's instant reaction was to shout, "No! It's none of your business!" Mr. Barab's position, expressed in his inimitable fashion, was that it was not the performer's job to try to *teach* the audience, nor was it the audience's responsibility to try to pass some sort of test in rhythm recognition. If he, the composer, had done his job well, and had organized and manipulated his musical materials in a compelling fashion, the music would "work," and the audience would enjoy it.

It's sad but true that many people denigrate and distrust their own reactions to classical music out of fear that they don't "know enough," and that other, more sophisticated folks know more. When people leave the movie theater they rarely hesitate to give their opinion of the movie, and it never occurs to them that they don't have a right to that opinion. And yet after most classical music concerts you can swing your program around from any spot in the lobby and hit a dozen perfectly capable and intelligent people issuing apologetic disclaimers: "Boy, I really loved that—but I'm no expert" or "It sounded pretty awful to me, but I don't really know anything, so I guess I just didn't get it."

At least those people showed up. Many others are too intimidated to attend classical concerts at all.

It's human nature to want to know more, and to try to understand and explain our experiences and reactions. And there's no denying that the more we know about music—as with cooking, or gardening, or football—the more levels of enjoyment are available to us, and the better we're able to recognize great achievement. Do we have to know the Latin names of flowers—or the English names, for that matter—to be moved by the beauty of a garden? No. Do we have to know about blocking schemes and "defensive packages" to be excited when our team scores a touchdown? No. But we find these things *interesting*. They add to our appreciation.

I'm all for knowledge—I've spent most of my career as a musician and commentator trying to help people learn more about music, and to remove any obstacles to the enjoyment of it. The Classical Music Insecurity Complex is a barrier of discomfort. Experience, exposure, and familiarity play critical roles in helping to lower that barrier, and a little learning, along with basic explanations of technical terms and concepts, can be of great value.

What is not of value and is in fact completely off-putting and counterproductive, is the kind of introductory concert talk, review, or program note that uses technical terms rather than plain English to explain other technical terms and to "describe" musical works. Program notes that use phrases like "the work features a truncated development with chromatic modulations to distant keys and modally inflected motivic cells," for example, do not exactly help to break down barriers and put people at ease.

Perhaps it's overly optimistic of me, but I still cling to the hope that, with the right approaches and experiences, longtime sufferers will feel sufficiently encouraged to go ahead and jettison the CMI Complex outright. I'd like the legions of actual and potential classical music lovers to believe that, like my friend the scientist, they hear more than they can name, and that the very point of listening to great music is to be moved, not to put names on what moves you.

I. CLASSICAL MUSIC

Classical Music

It remains a struggle to define the term "classical music." Some people call it "concert music," which seems a little too broad, or "art music," a little too exclusive, or "serious music," which is an insult to every other kind of music. It's often easier to say what classical music is not: it's not any one of the countless different styles of music that fall in the general category of "pop" music. Recently, though, I heard a definition that I like: "text-based music." The presence of a composed musical text, and the required fidelity to the details of that text, are in fact the central features of classical music. And where a text exists, the music has no expiration date. Interpretations of Beethoven's Fifth Symphony, for example, may change. But the text of the music, the notes themselves, will remain unchanged forever, which is why the music as Beethoven composed it can endure forever.

Music and Time

We know that music can give meaning to time: if all the interwoven elements in a piece of music mean something—if they remind, reflect, comfort, inspire, or excite—then by definition the time it takes for them to do all that will mean something, too. When I played in the National Symphony Orchestra in Washington, D.C., years ago, I used to have a little joke. Before we began a lengthy symphony, I'd turn to my colleague on stage and say, "See you in 45 minutes." A piece of music *must* take a certain amount of time; there's no way around it. But within that self-contained fragment of time, within that separate little world of music—if it's good music—time can be spent, saved, arranged, and manipulated so that the passage of time makes sense, so that the time itself is meaningful.

Pieces, Not Parts

It's hard to write a good piece of music, a piece whose elements fit together in ways that make sense, that keep our interest, and that leave us feeling that the time spent listening has been worthwhile. I once asked the composer Max Raimi what he thought of a certain other composer's music. He replied that her music had interesting sounds, textures, and moments, but that it tended to lack three things that he considered very important: a beginning, a middle, and an end. The novelist Joseph Conrad once wrote that human beings have as great a need for narrative as for breath. But our need for *narrative* is not restricted to the realm of literature, and when we listen to a piece of music, the only reason we're going to care in the least about where we are now, is if we have a sense that where we are now follows in some discernible way from where we've been, and if our interest is piqued as to where we may be going. I suppose you could make the case that life itself is nothing but a series of moments, some related, some not. But even if that rather limited description is true for life, it's not a recipe for compelling music. And I don't know about you, but when I read a review saying that a piece is constructed of 'shimmering hazes of sound,' or 'a parade of fascinating effects,' or 'random rhythmic bursts and captivating colors,' I'm usually pretty sure that it's a piece I'm not terribly interested in hearing. All good pieces contain captivating sounds or colors of one kind or another. But "parts is parts," to quote an old hamburger commercial, and good composers write coherent pieces, not collections of interesting materials. Many years ago I brought an ill-fitting suit home from college. My father took one look, chuckled, and said, "That's a nice piece of material. It's too bad somebody didn't make a suit out of it."

"Soothing" Music

When "classical" public radio stations surveyed their audiences some years back, the most common answer to the question, "Why do you listen to classical music?" was, "Because it's soothing." Now think of Beethoven for a moment, the man whose very name defines "classical music" for many people. He wrote music that sends the soul soaring, that plumbs the depths of human despair, that shatters silence with violent assaults. Beethoven's Fifth, for example, is many things, but *soothing*? Well, "soothing" sometimes does just mean soothing—a few moments of *Moonlight*, perhaps, after a *Twilight of the Gods* kind of day. But my theory is that what people most often really mean by "soothing" is "reassuring." Great classical music is reassuring in that listeners know that their musical expectations will be fulfilled; that there remains order, beauty, dependability, familiarity, and meaning in our disturbed and disturbing world.

Taste vs. Judgment, Good Pieces vs. Bad

We tend to be reluctant these days to say that one piece of music is better than another or that one composer is better than another. Often this reluctance is a good thing, especially if the ranking serves no useful purpose, and because "better" is sometimes hard to define. But sometimes the reluctance is a mistake, and it's a mistake based on confusing taste with judgment. You're certainly free, for example, to prefer the works of Antonio Salieri to those of Wolfgang Amadeus Mozart, if that's your taste. But if you say that Salieri is a better composer than Mozart, you're simply wrong. And you're not wrong based on taste, you're wrong based on the combined judgment of countless experts and countless audiences. Molière once said, "Anyone can be an honorable man, and yet write verse badly." Well, no one would dispute that there are many honorable men and women who write music. But if there are such things as "good pieces" or "great pieces," then there must also be such things as bad pieces. There must be pieces that don't work very well or don't work at all, pieces that don't offer much even to the most open-minded and honorable of music lovers. The passage of time can certainly help give perspective. Do you agree with the judgment that the two greatest composers of the late Baroque period were Bach and Handel? Well, that means, unavoidably, that the rest of the late Baroque composers were less great. And some weren't very good at all. But it's worth remembering that we don't have to apply our judgment only to composers who are dead.

Density of Brilliance

A scientist I know was talking about great works of literature, and she said that what characterized them was a "density of brilliance." What a wonderful phrase. And how perfect, too, for great works of music. In any five minutes, or any two minutes, of a musical masterpiece we can find a veritable parade of brilliant ideas. What's interesting is that the brilliant ideas don't always sound brilliant. Sometimes they just sound right. Absolutely right. And even inevitable. But they weren't inevitable. They were inventions, and they were choices, and in each and every case they started out as blank spaces on composition paper. We sometimes forget, I think, that at every single moment in the composition of a piece a composer has to choose what comes next from an infinite array of invented possibilities. The choices of great composers always *seem* to have been inevitable—and that's what makes those composers great.

Listening to Classical Music

Different people listen to classical music in different ways and for different reasons. Some people have it on in their homes during meals, some while they're relaxing or *in order* to relax, and some all the time. Some people like to have classical music on in the background while they're working, and some people absolutely *can't* work that way, and only want to hear classical music when they can pay close attention, whether it's at home or in a concert hall. And the *same* people will listen to music in different ways and for different reasons depending on when and where they're listening. Those of us who play classical music for a living sometimes get a little huffy at the thought of people "relaxing" to great music. But that's when we need to check our PCMSQs—our Personal Classical Music Snootiness Quotients—and remind ourselves that there's no single right way to listen to classical music. Our needs and intentions naturally vary in different situations, and everyone is entitled to listen in one way at one time and in another way at another. People listen to classical music in elevators, it's true; but couples kiss in elevators, too, and at airport ticket counters, and I doubt it would occur to those couples that they've exhausted all the possibilities for kissing.

Empathy

Why is it that when we're feeling sad, or lonely, or downright miserable, we're usually drawn to music that somehow reflects our mood, rather than music that might jar us out of it? Personally, I think in our darker moods, we're not looking to be told that everything's really just fine in this bright and shiny world and that we needn't, or shouldn't, be feeling the way we do. We try not to tell our children that their feelings are "wrong," so why should we tell ourselves such things? What we're rather seeking is understanding of our all-too-human feelings, and empathy as we face the inevitable trials and tribulations of life. Music that reflects our gloomier moods tells us, far more directly and more beautifully than mere words, that our humanity is shared, our feelings understood. And from understanding and empathy come hope and comfort.

That Modern Stuff

There are many people who say they love classical music, but not "that modern stuff"—even though some of "that modern stuff" is well over a hundred years old. Sometimes the term "modern" is just a stand-in for "unfamiliar," and it's true that some listeners have no appetite or patience for music that's unfamiliar, and aren't even willing to give it a try. That may be their loss, but then again we're all free to stick to what we know and love. I think that more often, though, what people mean by "modern stuff" is simply music that doesn't seem to make sense. It may make sense on paper, but for all too many of us it doesn't make sense to the ear. And I'm afraid there's been too much of that kind of music foisted on the public over the past century, so that, unfortunately, the many contemporary composers who are writing *good* music often get lumped in with those who are writing "that modern stuff." And that's everybody's loss.

All You Need Is Love

We often wonder, "Which pieces by contemporary composers will be familiar to classical music lovers fifty, a hundred, two hundred years from now?" Well, it's not foolproof, but one pretty good indicator is that if a piece remains unloved after fifty years, or has entirely dropped out of sight, it's not likely to be in the standard repertoire after a hundred years. *Love* is the key word. It's all very well for critics to admire a composer's theories or philosophy, or to marvel at the unusual sound effects of a piece, its shocking novelties, and the cleverness of its rhythmic complexities and hidden mathematical structure. But in the long run, the music that lasts is the music that moves people, the music that people want to hear again and again over the course of their lives—the music, in other words, that people love.

Malaria – and Music

My cousin Stephen Hoffman and his wife, Kim Lee Sim, are scientists, and they've developed a malaria vaccine that may one day save millions of lives. It's taken them years of intense effort and many disappointments along the way, but the results could one day change the world. And what do I do? I play music. Wars rage and diseases spread, all over the world, and I play music. Sometimes I feel like Nero—fiddling while Rome burns. Then again, I like to believe that for most people, and except for those in the very direst of circumstances, the purpose of life is not simply to stay alive. And the riches that music has to offer, whether in times of great sorrow or great joy, are both incalculable and irreplaceable. "Without music," said Nietzsche, "life would be a mistake." I comfort myself by believing Nietzsche was right, and when I actually try to imagine a world, or a life, without music, I know he was right.

Program Notes – George Bernard Shaw

If you're allergic to highly technical program notes for classical music concerts, you're not alone. Most musicians I know find such notes boring and irrelevant, and most non-musicians find them useless, and seriously off-putting. Well, it turns out it's an old problem, as I discovered when I read a wonderful essay by George Bernard Shaw from 1896. "[Thirty years ago]," Shaw wrote, "the average program-mist would unblushingly write, 'Here the composer...has abruptly introduced the dominant seventh of the key of C Major into the key of A flat, in order to recover, by a forced modulation, the key relationship proper to the second subject of a movement in F: an awkward device which he might have spared himself by simply introducing his second subject in its true key of C.'" Shaw's verdict on the value of such a passage? "I could teach [this style] to a poodle in two hours." My own advice, if you come across program notes like these? Ignore them. First of all, it's the annotator's fault that the notes are uninteresting and annoying, not yours. If you're not a mathematician, why on earth should you be expected to find a page full of equations interesting or comprehensible? But more importantly, when you ignore such program notes, you're not missing anything. It's the *composer's* job to understand and manipulate the technical materials of music—the composer's job to write music that's effective when we hear it, not when we read about it. And if the piece we're hearing is incomprehensible and ineffective without an accompany-ing technical analysis, all it means is that the composer hasn't done his or her job very well.

Atonal Music

Atonal music is music that isn't written in a key, music that doesn't follow the tra-ditional rules of harmony. But although the term "atonal" tells us what a piece *isn't*, it doesn't tell us what it is. Many different styles and musical languages, whether harsh or lush, cool or intense, simple or complex, can be described as atonal. *Tonal* music unfolds with a built-in logic established by centuries of development. But composers writing in atonal languages must create their own logic, and that's dif-ficult to do. When it's done badly, the music seems incoherent at best, unpleasant or annoying at worst, and we feel that our time, so precious to us, has been wasted. When it's done well, the logic makes itself understood, and the atonal musical language, though perhaps unfamiliar, becomes comprehensible and convincing. We hear patterns that make sense, patterns that can lead to drama, narrative, and emotional impact.

Progress – Part 1

In fields such as science, engineering, and medicine, we're used to achievements that represent progress, progress that is obvious and indisputable. We know more than we did before, and we do things better. But in the field of music, progress has at times been a misleading concept. Is there such a thing as becoming a better violinist than Jascha Heifetz, a better cellist than Mstislav Rostropovich, a better teacher than the great teachers of days gone by? I don't think so. For me as a musician, and as a teacher of music, progress doesn't mean getting better than someone else, or better than those who came before. It means getting better than I used to be, and trying to approach the level of those musicians and teachers I admire the most. It means, in other words, getting, in my own way, where others have already gotten.

Progress – Part 2

All right, then: for performing musicians and music teachers, the concept of progress can be misleading. We can strive in our own ways to emulate the masters who've preceded us, but it's usually a mistake to think there's such a thing as being better than those masters. But for composers, mistaken concepts of progress can be downright dangerous. Human nature doesn't change, nor do the reasons people listen to music. We may at different times experience a thousand different feelings or ideas in music, but we always seek meaning; we seek music that *awakens* feelings and ideas, and that organizes time in ways that make sense to us. In other words, although musical styles may change, there is no such thing as progress in the essential goals of music. But some composers forget that, and either forget or ignore human needs and human limitations. The result? Bad music. Time is our greatest treasure, and bad music wastes it.

Geniuses – Ordinary and Magical

The mathematician Mark Kac once tried to describe the extraordinary genius of the physicist Richard Feynman. "There are two kinds of geniuses," Kac wrote. "The 'ordinary' and the 'magicians.' An ordinary genius is a fellow that you and I would be just as good as, if we were only many times better. There is no mystery as to how his mind works. It is different with the magicians... the working of their minds is for all intents and purposes incomprehensible." In the world of classical music we've all been the beneficiaries of the work of *many* geniuses—great performers, certainly, and especially those great composers whose works have been loved for generations and will be loved for endless generations to come. But here's an interesting question: on that long list of musical geniuses, who would you classify as "ordinary" geniuses, and who would you consider the "magicians"? And not just "who," but "why." Something to think about.

Indispensable Three

It's always fun to propose lists of the "ten best" of something—or the ten worst of something, for that matter. But when it comes to thinking about composers of classical music, there's a word I like better than "best," and that word is *indispensable*. And the number I have in mind isn't ten, but rather three. Which three composers are indispensable to any account of those who have made the greatest contributions to the living repertoire of classical music? And not as a matter of personal taste, but as a matter of judgment. You're not allowed to choose Ishkabibble von Finkelbottom, for example, just because he's your favorite composer. Or to put it another way: the Yellowstone super-volcano is about to explode, and the escape pod leaving Earth forever only has data-storage room for the music of three composers. Who gets to go? For me, the answer is easy: Bach, Mozart, and Beethoven. How about for you?

Great Artists, Lousy People

There are many great creative artists, including great composers, who have been mediocre human beings, not to mention those who have been downright reprehensible human beings, or human beings whose private views we would find reprehensible if only we knew what they were. It's less troubling with minor or insignificant artists—if we don't like who they are, or were, we can comfortably ignore them, and it's no great loss. But genius complicates things. Pablo Picasso's granddaughter said he "crushed" women onto his canvas and bled them dry. Richard Wagner was an anti-Semite of the first order. Should we vow never to look at the works of Picasso again, never to listen to the works of Wagner? Those would be valid choices, certainly, but they'd be costly ones. And I should add that they'd only be valid as personal choices, not as choices to be imposed on others. Each of us will inevitably approach these problems from a different point of view, assigning importance in different proportions and often finding ourselves making choices based on emotion and personal taste rather than on a rationally consistent philosophy.

Musical Borrowing

For centuries, composers of classical music have been borrowing and adapting ideas and styles from popular music. Renaissance composers, for example, based Roman Catholic masses on popular tunes. Later composers made liberal use of folk tunes and folk styles of all kinds, and modern composers have borrowed freely from ragtime, jazz, and blues, among many other popular styles. But here's what we sometimes forget: it's always worked in the other direction, as well. The chords and harmonic progressions that you'll hear in ragtime and jazz, for example, or in French café music, or in Afropop, were almost all developed over hundreds of years in the Western classical tradition. And if "it don't mean a thing if it ain't got that swing," try listening to the wild syncopations in some of the motets and madrigals from the 1400s and 1500s. In music, everything belongs to everybody, and that's a beautiful thing.

Pronunciation

Classical music lovers tend to worry about correct pronunciation, so here are a few refreshers that I hope will be helpful. In America, people who play the flute call themselves flutists, not flautists, and we who play the viola, which is pronounced vee-ola, not vye-ola (unless you're referring to the name, Viola), are called violists, pronounced vee-olists. Handel's *Messiah* was written by Handel, not Hondle, and though you can say Haendel if you're feeling German, Handel himself changed it to Handel (pronounced like handle), so I'd stick with that. Mozart is Moh-tzart, not Moh-zart, but before we get too snooty about it, we might remember that the French, for example, *don't* say Moh-tzart, they say Moh-zahr. And speaking of the French, do go ahead and pronounce the Z's in Berlioz and Boulez, and don't be fooled by the letters e-n-c: Francis Poulenc is Poo-lank (rhymes with bank), not Poo-lahnk. Penderecki is pronounced Pender-etskee, not Pender-ekkee, but otherwise I'm afraid when it comes to Polish and Czech, you're on your own.

Opus Numbers

Opus is the Latin word for "work," as in "a work for violin and orchestra." Opus numbers are numbers assigned to a composer's works to indicate usually either their order of composition or the order of their publication. Sometimes a group of related pieces is published as a set with one opus number, in which case each piece in the set is given an additional identifying number. Beethoven's Op. 59, No. 3, for example, is the third of three string quartets published together as Op. 59. In 1950 a musicologist named Wolfgang Schmieder published a monumental catalogue of J. S. Bach's works, but Schmieder organized the catalogue by category, that is, by type of composition, not by date of composition. The catalogue is known in German as the Bach-Werke-Verzeichnis, or BWV, and that's why you often see Bach's works listed in programs with their BWV numbers. Mozart's works have "K" numbers, for Ludwig Köchel, who published a chronological Mozart catalogue in 1862, and Schubert's compositions are often given "D" numbers, for the chronological catalogue first published in 1951 by the Viennese scholar Otto Erich Deutsch. And if you're wondering why there's no special letter for Beethoven, it's because Beethoven, pioneer in this area as in so many others, was the first major composer who systematically assigned opus numbers to his own works.

Program Music

"Program music" is instrumental music that attempts to tell a story, paint a scene or picture, or convey impressions of a character, place, or event. But no matter how sonically descriptive, music is always open to a range of interpretations, sometimes far removed from the composer's intentions, and no two people will ever hear the same work in exactly the same way. I'll go further: in most cases, without descriptive titles, we wouldn't have the first foggiest clue of what an instrumental piece was supposed to be about. And what does "about" even mean, when it comes to music? It's almost always a term to be avoided—and not just for program music. I hear sadness? You hear quiet resolution. You hear the rain on the mountaintops? I hear a three-year old splashing in the mud. I have no right to impose my "about" on you, nor should you try to impose yours on me—even, by the way, if you're a radio announcer.

Debussy – "Descriptive" Music

Franz Liszt coined the term "program music," and said that when a piece has a program, or story, the musical ideas should clearly reflect the unfolding of the story— although that's the same Franz Liszt who attached a program to his symphonic poem *Les Préludes* long *after* he had actually written the music. Claude Debussy certainly gave his pieces picturesque titles—think of Prel*ude to the Afternoon of a Faun*, or *La Mer* ("The Sea"), just to name a couple of the most famous ones—but here's what he himself wrote about so-called "descriptive" music: "Does one convey the mystery of a forest by measuring the height of its trees? And isn't it rather its unsoundable depth that stirs the imagination?"

Schumann – Picturesque Titles

Like many 19th-century composers, Robert Schumann often gave his works picturesque titles. Schumann's *Scenes from Childhood*, for example, a set of pieces for solo piano, includes pieces with titles such as "Pleading Child," and "Frightening." How literally should we take these titles, and perhaps the picturesque titles of other composers' works? Well here's what Schumann himself wrote: "I have seldom come across anything more clumsy and shortsighted than what [the critic] Rellstab wrote about my *Scenes from Childhood*. He supposes I took some screaming child as my model and then tried to find the right notes. It was the other way round. Though I do not deny I saw a few children's faces in my mind's eye while I was composing; but the titles were added later, of course, and are really no more than slight pointers to the way of interpreting and playing the pieces."

Style Fights – Silly, but Productive

It occurs to me, when considering the history of music, that the endlessly recurring and often bitter critical fights over musical styles and trends have actually been quite productive, if only because they've acted as spurs for composers in supposedly opposing camps to produce their best work. It turns out, happily, that later generations usually have no trouble enjoying all the styles in question, and the old disputes just seem silly to them. "I am obliged to admit," wrote the composer Rossini, "that when I read big, ugly words such as *Progress, Decadence, Future, Past, Present, Convention*, etc., my stomach heaves with a motion I find extremely difficult to repress...and although I was an accomplished singer of Italian *bel canto* before becoming a composer...I agree with the philosophy of the great poet who declares that...'All styles are good/Except the *tedious* style.'"

Crescendo

How often have you come across a phrase such as, "the applause reached a crescendo," or "the battle reached a crescendo"? Well, the problem is that you can't, in fact, *reach* a crescendo. And that's because a crescendo is a process; it's the process of growing, of getting louder. The word comes from the Italian *crescere*, "to grow." And although you can certainly make a crescendo from soft to loud, you can also make a crescendo from extremely soft to very soft, or from very soft to moderately soft. What you can reach, if things get loud or exciting enough, is a climax. But climax and crescendo are not the same thing: it's the crescendo that can *get* you to the climax. I should mention that if at some point you've slipped up and misused crescendo, you can perhaps be comforted by the fact that otherwise excellent writers misuse it all too often. I was re-reading *The Great Gatsby*, for example, and sure enough, there was F. Scott Fitzgerald "reaching a crescendo" on page 55. Or thinking he was, anyway.

High and Low in Music

In music, the terms "high" and "low," as in "high notes" and "low notes," "high pitched" and "low pitched," are metaphors. High and low may be used to describe frequencies, or the relative position of printed notes on a musical staff, but printed notes are themselves merely symbols, not sounds, and frequencies and their measurements don't actually have height. We know that in reality, high notes are not physically higher, not farther from the surface of the earth, than low notes. But in English, high and low are the best terms we've been able to come up with to give us mental images of pitch. We forget that high and low are just metaphors, but we all agree on what they mean, so they've become indispensable. And since that's the case, let's keep hoping that when the soprano sings her highest notes and reaches the heights of passion at the high point of the opera—we won't be let down.

Repeats

Composers often call for *repeats* in their music, that is, for whole sections of their pieces to be played twice. And the question is: what's the point? One answer is that the repeat helps the listener remember the musical material. But more important, I think, is that the second time through a section always has different meaning, precisely because we've already heard it once. A return, no matter if it's to a person, a place, or an experience, always feels very different from a first meeting. Think of a second bite of cake, or a second kiss. When we've had the first, we know what to expect. Anticipation of the second adds meaning to the experience, and if our expectations are pleasurable, their satisfaction adds yet more levels of meaning. Furthermore, *after* a musical repeat, the music takes a different direction from the direction it took after the first time through, and that lends added meaning, retro-spectively, to what we've just heard.

Live Performance

I play concerts for a living, so you wouldn't think I'd need reminding of the dra-matic difference between listening to a recording and hearing a live performance. But it was as an audience member, not long ago, not as a performer, that I had my reminder, and it was a pretty spectacular one, because I was lucky enough to attend a concert by the Chicago Symphony Orchestra. The orchestra played music by Franz Schubert and Carl Maria von Weber, and they premiered a wonderful new piece by my friend Max Raimi. Max plays viola in the Chicago Symphony, and he also happens to be one of the most gifted contemporary American composers. Now it's true that not every orchestra is the Chicago Symphony, but it's also true that the level of playing in professional orchestras all around the country is remarkably high, and I'll bet that within twenty-five miles of wherever you live there's a sym-phony orchestra that plays beautifully. My advice? Buy a ticket and go hear them. And I promise it'll be a thrill.

Desert Island Music Choices – Part 1

It's an old question: if you were going to be dropped off on a desert island and you could only take a few recorded pieces of music with you, what would they be? For me, the first piece on the list is easy: Mozart's *Marriage of Figaro*. The music itself is beautiful and funny and brilliant and heart breaking and anything else you could possibly desire, but I'd also want *The Marriage of Figaro* with me for the company. How could I feel lonely if I were sharing the island with Susanna, Figaro, Cherubino, and all the other interesting characters in the opera? After the Mozart it gets trickier, but there are at least two other pieces that I couldn't bear to leave behind, pieces that combine moments of great beauty with warmth, humor, and indescribable tenderness: Felix Mendelssohn's Overture and Incidental Music to *A Midsummer Night's Dream*, and Maurice Ravel's opera *L'enfant et les sortileges*. I might be marooned, but I'd be smiling a lot.

Desert Island Music Choices – Part 2

I've mentioned a few pieces of music I'd like to have with me if I were marooned on a desert island, but I thought perhaps I should also list a few pieces I would definitely *not* want along. I'm assuming my island would be surrounded by water, so right away Debussy's *La Mer* would be out. It's a wonderful piece, but it would be superfluous, to put it mildly, and probably pretty annoying, under the circumstances. The same, of course, goes for Handel's *Water Music*. And since I doubt I'd be in the mood for irony, *Victory at Sea*, by Richard Rodgers, would also get left behind. On the theory that I wouldn't much enjoy being reminded of my predicament, I'd avoid Schubert's "Wanderer Fantasy," and since it's possible I might want to go for a swim, or try to catch a fish, the John Williams soundtrack from "Jaws" would most definitely get the kibosh. Gershwin's *An American in Paris* would be too painful a fantasy, and Beethoven's "Tempest" Sonata would just be looking for trouble. But I think you'll agree that the piece to be avoided at all costs would have to be Sergei Rachmaninoff's *Isle of the Dead*.

Waltz

When the dance known as the waltz first became popular in Europe in the late 1700s, it was considered by many to be the ultimate in lewdness and licentiousness. One German observer in the 1790s wrote: "The…dancers…went whirling about in the most indecent positions; the [men's] supporting [hands] lay firmly on the breasts, at each movement making little lustful pressures; the girls went wild and looked as if they would drop…" A few years later the London Times proclaimed it their duty "to warn every parent against exposing his daughter to so fatal a contagion." Well, the warnings didn't work, and not only that, the waltz became respectable. With the music of the Viennese composer Johann Strauss, Jr., the waltz reached the pinnacle of its popularity, and in 19th-century Vienna you could find enormous dance halls packed with thousands of people dancing the waltz.

Abraham Lincoln, Music Lover

I wonder if you knew that our sixteenth president was a great music lover. Not only that, he was an opera lover. On his way to Washington for his first inauguration, Lincoln stopped in New York City and attended a performance of Verdi's *A Masked Ball*—which is a little spooky, since that opera features the assassination of a political figure—and for the festivities at his second inauguration, he ordered a performance of Friedrich von Flotow's opera *Martha*. During the Civil War, the president went to the opera some thirty times, and to those who criticized him for doing so, he replied, "I must have a change, or die." His tastes were in fact wide ranging: he also liked popular songs and sentimental ballads, and he was partial to the piano music of Louis Moreau Gottschalk. One of Lincoln's favorite songs, believe it or not, was "Dixie," and after the war he happily proclaimed it "federal property."

R&J

There have been at least 24 operas based on Shakespeare's *Romeo and Juliet*. Most of those operas, however, are now almost completely forgotten. Of the very few well-known Romeo and Juliet operas, there's one in French, Charles Gounod's *Roméo et Juliette*; one in Italian, Vincenzo Bellini's *I Capuletti e i Montecchi* ("The Capulets and the Montagues"); and one in German, *Romeo und Julia*, by Heinrich Sutermeister, a 20th-century Swiss composer who was perfectly happy to have his opera premiered and performed in Nazi Germany during World War II. The English composer Frederick Delius wrote an opera called *A Village Romeo and Juliet* that was inspired by the play but not actually based on it, and a fellow named Leonard Bernstein wrote an updated, musical version of R&J called *West Side Story* that you may have heard of. The great non-operatic Romeo and Juliets include a "dramatic symphony" by Berlioz, a "fantasy-overture" by Tchaikovsky, and a full-length ballet by Prokofiev. No happy endings to be found in any of these works, I'm afraid, but lots of wonderful music.

Counterpoint

Counterpoint, also called *polyphony*, is the art, in musical composition, of combining two or more simultaneous lines of music. The word counterpoint comes from the Latin *punctus contra punctum*, meaning "note against note," and the adjective derived from the word counterpoint is *contrapuntal*. Now you might ask, why isn't it called contrapuntal writing when a melody is combined with an accompaniment? The answer is that in contrapuntal writing, the simultaneous musical lines are distinct and independent—each is a theme or melody that could stand alone. The trick, or rather the art, is that the lines are designed so that they sound good together. Think of a fugue by Bach, or even a simple round like "Row row row your boat." Each musical line keeps its individual identity, but the lines also act collectively, playing off one another and combining to create harmonies. Fugues, rounds, and canons are all contrapuntal forms.

Figured Bass – Continuo

In chamber music from the Baroque period, the written parts for keyboard instruments such as the harpsichord and organ often consisted of merely a bass line, with numbers written under the notes. Such a bass line was called a "figured bass," and the numbers, or figures, indicated which chords the keyboard player was expected to fill in *above* the bass, while at the same time improvising melodies (or countermelodies) to go along with what the other instruments were playing. The keyboard part was usually reinforced by a low instrument like the cello or bassoon doubling the bass line, and the resulting whole accompanying part—keyboard plus low instrument—was called the *basso continuo*, "continuous bass," or, for short, just *continuo*. So when you hear a Baroque piece described, for example, as a "trio sonata for flute, violin, and continuo," remember that, in this case, two plus one equals four: the continuo isn't an instrument, it's a *part*, and with two instruments playing it.

Finales

Throughout the eighteenth and nineteenth centuries in classical music, the final movements of instrumental pieces, the *finales*, were almost always in fast tempos, and they usually ended loud and emphatically. No matter where the rest of the piece had taken us, the finale was meant to provide a resolution, a sense that we'd just heard a complete work of art, a satisfyingly complete narrative, with a beginning, a middle, and, in no uncertain terms, an end. There was a kind of affirmative philosophy underlying the composer's work, and a projection of certainty: I know what I meant to say, I've said it, and there's value in my having said it. Over the last century or so, on the other hand—which is to say the age of world wars, atomic bombs, and televised catastrophes—as the world has changed, finales have changed. Composers in our age have felt much more willing, and sometimes even obligated, it seems, to end their pieces leaving listeners uncertain and disconcerted.

Folk Songs

For at least six hundred years, composers have been borrowing the melodies of folk songs and incorporating them into their compositions. And there's a good reason: they're good melodies; they're melodies that have stood the test of time, that have never lost their hold on people. And even when composers haven't borrowed actual folk melodies, they've often borrowed the style of folk melodies. In 1884 the composer Max Bruch, famous for *his* beautiful melodies, wrote a letter to his publisher, Fritz Simrock. Bruch wrote, "As a rule a good folk tune is more valuable than 200 created works of art. I would never have come to anything in this world, if I had not, since my twenty-fourth year, studied the folk music of all nations with seriousness, perseverance and unending interest. There is nothing to compare with the feeling, power, originality and beauty of the folksong..."

Serenade

Serenade is a musical term that has meant different things at different times. The term itself comes from the Italian *sereno*, which is from the Latin *serenus*, which means "serene." The original serenades—and by "original" I mean serenades from the 1500s and 1600s—were vocal pieces, usually meant to be sung outdoors in the quiet of the evening, and often aimed at the windows, and hearts, of beloved persons. Mozart and other composers of the Classical period (c. 1775-1820) turned the serenade into a multi-movement piece for various types and sizes of instrumental ensembles, and in that form the serenade is closely related to the form known as the "divertimento." From the 19th century to this day, composers have applied the title "serenade" at their pleasure to any number of different kinds of pieces, some light-hearted and some very serious, but very few requiring lovers and windows.

Christmas Carols

Nobody knows for certain where the word "carol" comes from. It may come from the Latin word "chorus," by way of the Greek "khoros"—both words having to do with dancing in a circle, probably while singing. Carol may also be related to the word "corolla," which in Latin originally referred to a circle of stones, or an enclosed circular space. In any case, by the 12th century, *caroler* was the common Old French word for "to dance," and in England by the 16th century, "caroll" had somehow come to refer to songs, and usually to Christmas songs in particular. These days the Christmas carolers who knock on your door tend to be polite and nicely groomed, but you may want to reflect on the thought that back in the Dark Ages and before, the original carolers were most likely out there in animal skins, dancing around in circles under the stars and singing songs that, to *our* ears, might sound quite peculiar.

Thanksgiving 1621

It was in November of 1621 that the Pilgrims of the Plymouth colony celebrated the first Thanksgiving. Existence was pretty bare bones in Plymouth in those days, and there certainly wasn't much going on musically. I find it fascinating to think about that in light of what was going on in Europe at the same time. By 1621, for example, the new musical form known as *opera* had been around for about twenty years, the instruments of the modern violin family were already almost 90 years old, and the system of writing music in major and minor keys had been firmly established for several decades. And it was in 1626, while the Pilgrims were still shivering in their cabins, that the first permanent orchestra in the Western world was established, in warmer buildings, at the court of Louis XIII of France. That orchestra was *Les 24 Violons du Roy*—The 24 Violins of the King.

Interesting Tempo and Expression Markings

The most common tempo markings in music are the words *allegro, adagio,* and *andante,* for (roughly) fast, slow, and medium. But often composers indicate expression along with tempo, and this is when foreign-language dictionaries can come in handy. I could make a long list of interesting tempo and expression markings, but here are two of my favorites: *Rasendes Zeitmass, Wild, Tonschönheit is nebensache.* "Racing tempo, Wild, Beauty of tone is irrelevant." That's Paul Hindemith's marking for the fourth movement of his Sonata for Solo Viola, Op. 25, No. 1. And here's Mozart having fun with the instructions for the last movement of his A Major flute quartet: *Rondieaoux: Allegretto grazioso, ma non troppo presto, però non troppo adagio. Così-così—con molto garbo ed espressione.* "Rondiaoo: A graceful allegretto, but not too fast, however not too slow. So-so—with great elegance and expression."

II. COMPOSERS

Composers' Lives – Part 1

Should we really care about the personal lives of the composers we admire? When we don't know anything about their lives, we certainly don't care. How many of us know a great deal about Monteverdi, or Palestrina? Or even Bach, or Beethoven? What we care about is the music. But still, we're curious, especially about composers whose work has meant a great deal to us, composers who seem to have understood our very hearts and souls. We have a slightly strange but very human need to try to be close to these people, even when they're long dead; to feel some sort of personal relationship, and perhaps even to thank them. We also often hope to gain insights into the music itself, the how and why of it. But that's a tricky business, especially since inner motivation is often only related to specific life experience in ways that are either very tangled or completely hidden.

Composers' Lives – Part 2

One of the perils of studying composers' lives is finding out that some of the people whose music we love and admire turn out to have been very *un*admirable human beings. A famous example in this category is Richard Wagner, an egomaniac and anti-Semite, among other things, but a man who wrote lots of exquisitely beautiful music. What are we to make of such jarring disjunctions? Should we throw out the music with the maniac? I don't have the answer. If your personal association with the music of Wagner is the memory of hearing it broadcast by the Nazis, that's one thing, and it's understandable that you'd never want to hear it again. The problem is that the beauty is real, and it will outlast us, all of us. My choice, for lack of a better one, is simply to use cases like Wagner's as occasions to marvel at the complexities and apparent contradictions of human nature, and to realize that there are some questions I just can't answer.

Composers and Mental Illness

It's popular, in some circles, to find links between creative genius and mental illness, and even to use mental illness to *explain* creative genius. When it comes to composers, Robert Schumann, who attempted suicide after years of inner torment, is usually put forth as Exhibit A, but others are often mentioned as well. My own view is that the so-called link is no link at all. Number one, I think you'd be hard-pressed to prove that the incidence of mental illness is any higher among great composers than among the general population, and number two, and more importantly, it's crucial to remember that those geniuses who suffered from mental illness created great works not *because* of their afflictions, but despite them. Not only should we admire their genius, in other words, we should admire their tenacity in the face of pain—their courage. Genius is disconcerting, because we can't explain it. But that doesn't mean we should try to cut genius down to size by forcing it into a category with illness.

Composers' Letters

It's true that, occasionally, the music that composers write reflects in some way what's been going on in their lives. But more often than not the music gives no clue, even in the broadest sense. For composers of past eras, it's their letters, much more than their compositions, that open windows into their private thoughts, and into the joys and struggles of their personal lives. The sheer number of letters that many composers wrote in the days before telephones and computers is astounding. Felix Mendelssohn, for example, is thought to have written between five and ten thousand letters during his lifetime, and his contemporary Franz Liszt undoubtedly wrote that many or more. Did they dash them off as quickly as we write emails? I don't know, but I often wonder how, with all that letter writing, people like Mendelssohn and Liszt ever had the time to compose music.

Composers' Friends and Colleagues

Isn't it wonderful to think that among the greatest composers of the 19th century—composers such as Berlioz, Schumann, Chopin, Mendelssohn, Liszt, Wagner, Brahms, Dvořák, and Tchaikovsky—there were many warm personal and musical relationships? And isn't it somehow almost breathtaking to picture figures we revere, immortal figures, sitting together in the same rooms, sharing lighthearted evenings? Robert Schumann, for example, wrote his piano quintet for his wife, Clara, a great piano virtuoso, and Clara played the first public performance of the piece. But the *very* first performance of the piece was at a party for friends, and the pianist for that performance was Felix Mendelssohn. At another private party, later, Clara played the piece, and here's what one of the guests wrote to the composer afterward: "Your Quintet, my very dear Schumann, pleased me greatly, and I asked your dear wife to play it twice... I see what path you want to follow, and can assure you that it's also mine – *there* is the only chance for salvation: beauty." And that guest's name was Richard Wagner.

Composers' Inspiration

Mozart, they say, could compose music while he was playing billiards. Rossini wrote that he had once composed an overture while standing in the water fishing and listening to his fishing partner discuss Spanish finance. Prokofiev and other composers were known to carry notebooks with them so that they could jot down musical ideas that came to them on long walks, while Aaron Copland, when asked once how he found the inspiration for his music, said that the secret to inspiration was to sit down and work. Some composers compose at their desks and some at the piano, and some do both. It's true that if you're composing music, sooner or later you have to spend time sitting down and writing it out—if these days you can *type* it out using computer software—but when and where, and *from* where composers get their creative ideas are questions for which the answers, even for any individual composer, will always vary.

Composers' Intent – An Aaron Copland Story

When musicians and music scholars prepare performances of works by dead composers, they often get stuck in arguments about what the composers' "original intent" was. And while I certainly recognize the importance of scholarly accuracy and authenticity, and of staying true to composers' wishes, I think that sometimes musicians forget that dead composers were once alive. Back in 1980 a pianist I know was preparing a performance of the Copland Piano Concerto, a performance that Aaron Copland himself was going to conduct, and the pianist had the opportunity to play the piece privately for the composer. After the first movement, Copland asked, "Why are you playing it so fast?" and the pianist, a little flummoxed, said that he was just trying to follow the printed metronome marking—to play at the tempo, in other words, that Mr. Copland had originally indicated when he published the piece. "You know," Copland replied, "I wrote this piece over fifty years ago. That may have been the tempo then, but this is the tempo now."

Composers of Chamber Music

Composers during the Baroque period, c. 1600-1750, wrote plenty of chamber music, especially trio sonatas and sonatas for such high-voiced instruments as the violin and the flute. But the chamber music repertoire that today's audiences are most familiar with probably begins with the piano trios and string quartets of Joseph Haydn (1732-1809). After Haydn, the floodgates opened. Mozart and Beethoven, for example, both composed vast quantities of great chamber music in a variety of forms, and with the exception of those who've specialized in opera, virtually all major composers of the 19th, 20th, and now 21st centuries, of whatever nationality, have made important, and in some cases extensive, contributions to the chamber music repertoire. Many composers wrote their chamber works with the intention of playing the pieces themselves in informal gatherings with their friends, which is undoubtedly why so much of the best chamber music is a delight to play.

Composers' Dreams

These days, with convenient hindsight, we take it for granted that good music lasts; that pieces that are well known now will remain well known for years, perhaps even for centuries to come. But I often wonder what was in the minds of the composers of centuries past whose music we still love. Composers such as Bach, Mozart, and Beethoven knew very well how good they were, and where they stood compared to other composers. They were too good *not* to have known. And they certainly studied the music of great composers who had come before them, so they knew that great music didn't just disappear with the deaths of those who had written it. But did it ever occur to Bach, Mozart, or Beethoven that their music would be played... *forever*? Did they hope for that? Dream of it? Could they even have conceived of the idea? I wonder.

Albeniz – Granados – Falla

The three most important Spanish composers of the late 19th and early 20th centuries are certainly Isaac Albeniz (1860-1909), Enrique Granados (1867-1916), and Manuel de Falla (1876-1946), all composers who brilliantly integrated Spanish folk influences into the Western classical tradition. All three were great pianists, and Albeniz and Granados in particular had important careers as solo performers. Both those men continued the long tradition of the composer/virtuosos who enriched the solo piano repertoire by writing pieces to showcase their own spectacular talents. Albeniz had perhaps the most colorful childhood of the three—he was performing in public by the age of nine, and by the age of fifteen he had played concerts all over the world—and Granados certainly had the most tragic end. In 1916 he played at the White House for Woodrow Wilson, but on his voyage back to Europe, his ship was torpedoed by a German U-Boat, and he and his wife both drowned.

Georges Auric

The French composer Georges Auric (1899-1983), was one of a group of avant-garde composers in Paris known as "Les Six," or "The Six," a group that also included Darius Milhaud and Francis Poulenc. The image of the romantic artist, tragic and solitary, had absolutely no appeal for Auric, and he wrote a number of works in collaboration with the other members of Les Six. In the 1930s Auric began composing music for films, and he eventually wrote the music for twenty-seven films in all. One song, "Where is Your Heart," from the 1952 film Moulin Rouge, is still probably Auric's best-known work. When he was in his sixties, Auric became the director of the Paris National Opera and the chairman of SACEM, the French version of ASCAP (American Society of Composers, Authors, and Publishers—a performance-rights organization), and in his later years he spent much of his time encouraging the efforts of young composers.

Johann Sebastian Bach

The essayist Lewis Thomas, musing on the question of what signals earthlings ought to broadcast to outer space in case alien life forms were listening, wrote, "I would vote for Bach, all of Bach, streamed out into space over and over again. We would be bragging, of course, but it is surely excusable to put on the best possible face at the beginning of such an acquaintance. Any species capable of producing the music of Johann Sebastian Bach cannot be all bad." Before we humans get too proud of ourselves, though, we should remember that, especially during the last twenty-five years of his life, Bach (1685-1750) was often underpaid, unrespected, and unhappy. The composer who's now universally revered was forced to supplement his earnings by playing weddings and funerals, and when his co-citizens weren't dying from disease in sufficient numbers, it was hard for him to make ends meet. He was expected to write enormous quantities of music, including new pieces every week, and he was required by his employers to teach music and Latin to children. Bach hardly traveled anywhere, but he did get to know the music of his contemporaries, so we can assume he was aware that *his* music was on a very different level. I hope that awareness was a comfort.

Bach's Sword

I believe our perceptions of J. S. Bach are skewed because of one painting. The only fully authenticated portrait of Bach shows him as an old man: stout, stolid, and bewigged. This is the Bach people recognize, the serious, even severe "old master" who played the organ and taught counterpoint to generations of children at the St. Thomas Church in Leipzig. Looking at this picture, it's not hard to imagine that Bach was great, but it is hard to imagine that he was ever young. Or slim. Or good-looking. But he was all those things, and more. He had twenty children, after all, and he didn't create them at the harpsichord. I like to remember that although Bach died at the age of sixty-five, he wasn't born at sixty-five, and that he wrote many of his great instrumental works when he was in his twenties and thirties. He always had quite a temper, drank lots of beer, was no stranger to scraps with his employers, and once even had a street fight in which, set upon by an angry bassoonist (Bach had insulted the man's playing, calling him a "nanny-goat bassoonist"), he defended himself by striking at the man with a sword.

Bach – Sacred, Secular, and Passionate

When people discuss J. S. Bach, words like "God" and "transcendence" tend to figure in the discussion. Gustav Mahler wrote that "in Bach, the vital cells of music are united as the world is in God," and Johann Wolfgang von Goethe said of Bach's music, "it was as if the eternal harmony was conversing within itself, as it may have done in the bosom of God, just before the creation of the world." This worshipful approach is understandable, and perhaps even inevitable, given Bach's awe-inspiring musical legacy, but the problem with such an approach is that we tend to forget that Bach was a human being. And for me, the key to understanding the greatness of Bach is to recognize that what propels his music, what infuses every note, is his very human passion. It's true that Bach wrote great quantities of profoundly moving sacred music. But the hallmark of his music, whether sacred or secular, is that it's always passionate. And it's important to remember that the emotions, or passions, that find their expression in religion, or in religious music, are universal emotions. They're variants—in religious clothing, you might say—of the feelings that are common to all people: love, longing, fear, devotion, peace, expectation, comfort, joy, and so forth. The distinguished literary critic Harold Bloom has made the point that "sacred" and "secular" are political and religious distinctions, not different *literary* categories. We might add that, at their core, sacred and secular aren't different musical categories, either. And Bach's music proves the point.

Pater - Botticelli - Bach

Walter Pater was an influential 19th-century English author and critic, and in 1870 he wrote a fascinating essay about the Italian Renaissance painter Sandro Botticelli. In one passage that particularly caught my eye, Pater wrote, "If [Botticelli] painted religious incidents, [he] painted them with an undercurrent of original sentiment, which touches you as the real matter of the picture through the veil of its ostensible subject." When I read this, I thought immediately of J. S. Bach. I have no reason to question Bach's own religious faith. But it's neither his faith nor the strength of his faith—a faith widely shared, after all—that distinguishes Bach from his contemporaries and from so many of his successors. It's his skill. His genius. Or perhaps, to be more specific, I should say it's the combination of some unnameable set of personal qualities with an unsurpassed, and largely unequaled, ability to turn feeling directly into music. One of Bach's greatest masterpieces is his *Mass in B Minor*. But the work is a setting of the Roman Catholic Mass, and Bach wasn't Catholic. He was Lutheran. The beliefs of Lutherans and Catholics differ in some important respects, so what beliefs was Bach expressing? What was he feeling as he wrote the Mass? And why is it that the *Mass in B Minor* often proves profoundly moving for people who feel no connection with the "ostensible subject" of the work, even for those who hold no religious beliefs at all? The answer certainly has something to do with Bach's "undercurrent of original sentiment"—his ability to find and to feel the universal in the particular, and to express his inner humanity in ways that reach infinitely outward.

Bach - Better

A colleague and I were listening to a Bach violin concerto on the radio some years back. After a while my colleague said, "You know, there are a thousand Baroque violin concertos. Why is it that this one is just…better?" Johann Sebastian Bach wrote sonatas, concertos, suites, preludes and fugues, overtures, oratorios, and cantatas—music in all the major forms of the Baroque era, with the exception of opera. But Bach himself didn't invent any of the forms he used. He used the forms he inherited, but he transformed them, with a kind of fearless creativity, and with expressive genius. He made them better. "It was not given to [Bach's predecessors] to quicken the forms with the spirit," wrote the philosopher, organist, and Bach scholar Albert Schweitzer. "If all their struggles toward the ideal were not to be in vain, a greater man had to come… Bach is thus a terminal point. Nothing comes from him; everything merely leads up to him."

Bach – Brandenburg Letter

Here's part of an interesting job application letter. It was originally in French:

"My Lord, As I had the honor of playing before Your Royal Highness... and as I observed that You took some pleasure in the small talent that heaven has given me for music, and [as] You honoured me with a command to send You some pieces of my composition, I now...take the liberty of presenting [you] with the present concertos...humbly praying You not to judge their imperfections by the severity of the fine and delicate taste that every one knows You to have for music ..." The letter, sent in the spring of 1721, was addressed to the Margrave of Brandenburg, and it was signed "Jean Sebastian Bach." Was the humility genuine? It's doubtful. And Bach didn't get the job. But it's certain that today the only reason anyone remembers the Margrave of Brandenburg is that his name became attached to six concertos by Johann Sebastian Bach.

Bach's St. Matthew Passion – and Felix Mendelssohn

J. S. Bach composed his *St. Matthew Passion* in 1727. But for the better part of a century after that, the piece essentially disappeared, unknown to all but a few specialists. One of those specialists was the composer Carl Friedrich Zelter, who was the music teacher of a boy named Felix Mendelssohn. Mendelssohn was only about fourteen when his grandmother gave him a copy of the full score of the *St. Matthew Passion*, a score she had borrowed from Zelter. The teenager immediately recognized the wondrous qualities of the music, and in 1829, about a month after his twentieth birthday—and 102 years after the first performance of the *St. Matthew Passion*—Felix Mendelssohn led a performance that reintroduced Bach's masterpiece to the musical public. And that reintroduction led to the rediscovery and reevaluation of many other works by Bach, and to his music finding the exalted place in the public's love and admiration that it's held ever since.

Seymour Barab

The American composer Seymour Barab started out as a pianist and organist, but as a teenager he took up the cello, and as a cellist he became a highly successful orchestra musician, founder of important string quartets, top commercial freelance player, champion of new music, and later, after mastering the viola da gamba, champion of old music. As a composer, Barab was incredibly fast and prolific, and he's especially known for his comic operas and children's operas. His opera *Little Red Riding Hood*, for example, has in some years been the most frequently performed opera in America. He also wrote countless songs and chamber music works, works that are always rhythmically complex and challenging to play, yet always somehow lighthearted and charming. Seymour Barab was born on January 9, 1921, and he died, at the age of 93, on June 28, 2014. I had the great good fortune to know him and to play his music, and I miss him.

Beethoven's Shadow

For convenience sake, the 19th century is usually known as the era of Romanticism in classical music. This is not necessarily wrong, but it certainly does lump a great number of composers of very different styles into one broad category. Another way to view the 19th century is simply as the era of Beethoven. And that's because *after* Beethoven, who died in 1827, all composers were seen and evaluated in Beethoven's light, or rather in his enormous shadow—seen by the public, and seen by themselves. Imagine the courage it took to write a symphony after hearing Beethoven's symphonies. Or a piano sonata, or a string quartet. The young Johannes Brahms once wrote, "I will never write a symphony... You have no idea how the likes of *us* feel when we hear the tramp of a giant like *him* behind us." For the less talented, perhaps it took not so much courage as obliviousness, and egotism. For the greatly talented: courage, confidence, and a sense that, 'I will never be Beethoven, but I can do my best, hope that I do something worthwhile on whatever path I take, and at the very least continue an important tradition with Beethoven as an ideal and an inspiration.' Then again, why should we limit our focus to the 19th century, or limit it at all? For the truth is that the world of classical music is still a world in many ways dominated, and illuminated, by Beethoven's brilliant shadow.

Berlioz on Beethoven

The words of the composer Hector Berlioz, writing about Beethoven on the occasion of the first "Beethovenfest," in Bonn, Germany, in 1845: "Today these thousands of men and women young or old...whom he has so often carried off on the wings of his thought to the highest regions of poetry; these devotees he has excited to the point of delirium; these jokesters he has amused by so many witty and unforeseen devices; these thinkers for whom he has opened up an endless expanse of dreams; these lovers he has stirred by awaking the memory of their first days of tender feeling; these hearts caught in the grip of an unjust fate, to whom his forceful sounds have given the strength for a momentary revolt, and who, rising up in outrage, have found voice to mix their cries of anger and pain with the furious sounds of his orchestra; these religious minds to whom he has spoken of God; these nature lovers for whom he has painted in such true colors the lazy and contemplative life in the country on beautiful summer days, the joys of the village, the terrors of the hurricane, and the consoling rays coming through the tattered clouds to bring a smile to the anxious shepherd and hope to the frightened laborer; it is now that all these intelligent and sensitive souls on whom his genius shined turn toward him as toward a benefactor and friend."

Beethoven – Portrait of a Successful Young Man

Some people may have the impression that Ludwig van Beethoven spent his entire life as a tormented, angry genius. He didn't. We don't know an enormous amount about Beethoven's childhood, but we do know that he was born in 1770; that as a boy he had lessons on the piano, violin, and viola; that by the age of eleven and a half he was acting as the deputy to the court organist at the court of the Elector of Cologne in his hometown of Bonn and had already starting composing; and that when he was twelve, a notice about him in a widely-read music magazine included the following sentences: "This youthful genius is deserving of help to enable him to travel. He would surely become a second Wolfgang Amadeus Mozart if he were to continue as he has begun." When he arrived in Vienna—he wasn't quite twenty-two—his reputation had preceded him, and he was immediately accepted into the best circles. There was very little in the way of public concert activity in Vienna at that time, but many citizens and members of the nobility held musical evenings, or salons, and Beethoven quickly became the darling of those salons. He played all over Vienna, and his listeners were flabbergasted—they'd never heard piano playing like his, and were especially amazed by his brilliant improvisations, by his *legato* playing (his ability to tie notes together with his "touch" in order to create a lyrical flow), and by what one friend called the "poetic fury" of his playing. And meanwhile, he was constantly composing. By his mid-twenties he was already a celebrity as both a performer and a composer, and before he turned thirty he had written his first ten piano sonatas, including the famous "Pathétique" sonata, his first five violin sonatas, two cello sonatas, eight piano trios, four string trios, his first six string quartets, his first two piano concertos, the First Symphony, the septet for strings and winds, and many other works. He had his choice of publishers for his works, and he had a generous retainer from a local prince, Prince Lichnowsky. This is a portrait, in other words, of an extremely successful young man, and of a man who knew where he stood. Beethoven was not exactly an easy-going fellow; we know from his own correspondence and from others' accounts that he had a temper, and that he was no stranger to arguments and mutual hurt feelings. But we certainly get no sense that, up until his mid-twenties, at least, he was suffering or feeling tormented. The torment—physical, because of terrible intestinal afflictions, and psychological, because of his hearing loss—came later.

Beethoven – Torment, Confidence, and Courage

By his late twenties, Beethoven had already suffered significant hearing loss, and by the time he reached his early thirties, it was clear that all attempts at reversing his hearing loss would fail. He kept right on composing, and for as long as he could he kept performing, but now he *was* a tormented, suffering genius. And although the primitive "cures" he endured might have alleviated his terrible abdominal distress a little bit, he was still in pain or acute discomfort much of the time—this is something you don't hear about much, because people tend to shy away from talking about diarrhea—and his deafness, with painful buzzing in his ears, kept getting worse. By 1814, he couldn't hear the orchestra when he was conducting, and although his student Czerny wrote that up until 1816 Beethoven could still hear himself play the piano "with the aid of machines," by 1817, when he was 47 years old, he was virtually stone deaf. What kept him going—what had already kept him going—was, quite simply, courage: courage born from his devotion to music and from his determination, in his own words, to have "brought forth all I felt within me."

Beethoven – Composing Without Sound

The common conception that it was somehow miraculous that Beethoven was able to compose even after he had lost his hearing is really a misconception. *Many* composers have been able to compose their works in their heads, hearing all the melodies, harmonies, and rhythms in their "mind's ear." They've sat at their desks and composed, or if they've sat at the piano it was to confirm what they'd already conceived, or to save time. Beethoven's mind's ear, his internal hearing, was at least as good, and probably far better, than that of any other well-trained musician. He could look at a score and hear it perfectly, and he could conceive musical ideas of great complexity in his head and commit them to paper the way others write down their thoughts in words. That Beethoven could not hear, therefore, was not a technical impediment, but a personal tragedy, a source of extraordinary anguish. It cut him off from society and from his friends, at least for a while; it meant that his brilliant performing career would be short-lived; and it meant that eventually he'd be deprived of the sensuous delights of *all* music, not just his own.

Leonard Bernstein

Leonard Bernstein was born in 1918 and died in 1990. His life was, more dramatically and certainly more publicly than most, a life of dualities. He grew up on music of the synagogue, but also on jazz. He was a conductor and also a composer. A classical composer and also a Broadway composer. A great teacher and completely devoted servant of music, and also an extraordinarily egotistical exhibitionist. A married man who loved his wife, the mother of his three children, but who was primarily attracted to men. A supremely self-indulgent human being and a remarkably generous one. He was staggeringly talented and successful, and also a person of painfully unfulfilled dreams. But here's the truth: as the years go by, his personal qualities will fade completely in importance, but his music and his legacy will last, and all that will matter is that Leonard Bernstein enriched the lives of millions and left the world a better place.

Bernstein – "Cool"

If you'd like a marvelous example of the genius of Leonard Bernstein, I recommend that you listen, or listen again, to the song "Cool," from *West Side Story*. Bernstein needed a song for the character Riff to sing to build up the tension before the "rumble," the gang fight between the Jets and the Sharks. If I told you his solution was to take Baroque counterpoint—a fugue, to be precise, with the fugue "subject" borrowed from a Beethoven string quartet—the syncopated rhythms of jazz, and the atonal twelve-tone technique of Arnold Schoenberg, and to mix them all together with a singer, a vibraphone, standard orchestral instruments, a drum set, and finger snapping, you'd probably say, "That sounds preposterous." And it does. But that's just what he did. And the result, which for anybody but Leonard Bernstein would have been inconceivable, was a fabulous Broadway show-stopper. Even the greatest hitters don't always hit home runs, and even geniuses don't always write masterpieces. But with "Cool," Bernstein hit it out of the park.

How I Won Ten Dollars from Leonard Bernstein

When I was a student at Juilliard, I learned the Viola Concerto by William Walton, and one evening I played through it for my violinist friend Alexis Galpérine. Alexis noticed that the Walton reminded him very much of the Violin Concerto in D Major by Sergei Prokofiev, and on closer examination we saw that there was no question that Walton had indeed patterned his concerto directly after the Prokofiev. Several years later I was playing in the National Symphony Orchestra when Leonard Bernstein came to conduct. The Walton was on the program with a guest soloist, and during the rehearsal Bernstein stopped and said, "I'll give ten dollars to anyone who can tell me which piece this Walton Concerto is directly modelled on." I raised my hand and said, "The Prokofiev D Major Violin Concerto." Bernstein looked at me and said, "Well," and paused. "I'm glad I didn't say fifty." And during the rehearsal break he paid up.

Vincenzo Bellini

Vincenzo Bellini—the composer of *Norma*, *La Sonnambula*, and *I Puritani*, to name a few of his best-known *bel canto* operas—is famous for the beauty of his melodies, but also for his ability to use melody to define character, express passion, and advance dramatic action. And he had nothing but disdain for what he called the "ridiculous rules" that some people thought composers should be obliged to follow when setting poetry to music. "Carve in your head in letters of brass," Bellini once wrote to a colleague. "An opera must draw tears, cause horror, bring death, by means of song... Poetry and music, to make their effect, must be true to nature, and that is all: anyone who forgets this is lost and will end by producing a dull, heavy work that can please only the pedants. It will never appeal to the heart... whereas if the heart is moved one will always be in the right..." Bellini was born in 1801, and he died in 1835, not quite thirty-four years old. *Bel canto* literally means "beautiful singing," and truth be told Bellini often gets pigeonholed as a composer of mere shallow vocal showpieces. But listen to a great soprano singing "Casta Diva," the most famous aria from *Norma*, and to a good performance of *Norma's* final scene, and I think you'll hear music of great depth; music of beauty, subtlety, and power that speaks to us—with words and without—about war, peace, hatred, intolerance, loyalty, regret, love between a woman and a man, love of a father for his daughter, and about the countless thoughts and feelings that have no names.

Ernest Bloch – Composer, Educator, Photographer

Ernest Bloch (1880-1959) was born in Geneva, Switzerland. He came to America in 1916 to pursue his career, but despite considerable early success he became disappointed and disillusioned and was planning to return to Europe. As a close friend of his wrote, "The burden of his lament…was that he had reached the end of his patience with rank commercialism, base intrigue, and flagrant hypocrisy. America apparently had no room for him, he had no use for America." It was a visit in 1922 to the Library of Congress, with its spectacular collections, its magnificent building, and its awe-inspiring view of the US Capitol, the Mall, and the monuments, that convinced Bloch to change his mind. He decided to stay in this country and to take American citizenship. Bloch was a famous and prolific composer: his catalogue includes such important works as *Schelomo* for cello and orchestra and *Avodath Hakodesh* ("Sacred Service," a setting of the service for the Jewish Sabbath). I'm particularly grateful, personally, for his superb works for the viola, his two violin sonatas, and his two piano quintets, especially the spectacular Piano Quintet No. 1. But he was also one of this country's most important educators, the founding director of the Cleveland Institute of Music and the first director of the San Francisco Conservatory of Music. A master photographer himself, Bloch was a friend of Ansel Adams and other famous photographers, and in a letter to Bloch in 1954, Adams wrote, "You may not have any recollection of it, but you considerably influenced the course of my work; I recall showing you some mountain photographs—at the time I was trying for dark skies and super-Wagnerian shadows—and you said something pointed about the lack of the feeling of *light* in the pictures. 'Mountains are Light!' you said. Well, that had quite an effect!!!" Upwards of five thousand of Bloch's own negatives, prints, and plates are in the collection of the Center for Creative Photography at the University of Arizona. A note on pronunciation: Bloch's native language was French, and he pronounced the final "ch" in his name as a "k." His American descendants pronounce the name quite simply "block."

Alexander Borodin

The composer Alexander Borodin was born in St. Petersburg, Russia, in 1833, and he became famous as one of the group of nationalistic Russian composers known as "The Five," a group that also included Modest Mussorgsky and Nikolai Rimsky-Korsakov. Borodin's best-known piece is undoubtedly the "Polovetsian Dances," from his opera *Prince Igor*, an opera that acquired a whole new public in the 1950s when its music was borrowed for the Broadway musical *Kismet*. It's curious that composing wasn't even Borodin's profession—it was his avocation. By profession, Borodin was a chemist, a very distinguished one who made a number of important contributions to the field. He was also a pioneer in the field of women's rights and women's education, and he was a founder of the School of Medicine for Women in St. Petersburg. He died in St. Petersburg, in 1887.

Giovanni Bottesini

Giovanni Bottesini was born in Crema, Italy, in 1821, and during his lifetime he was the most celebrated double bass virtuoso in the world. His concert tours took him all over Europe, and to Russia, Egypt, Cuba, Mexico, and the United States. As a child, he started on the violin, but when it was time to apply to the Conservatory of Milan for further studies, the only scholarships available were for bassoon and double bass. With just a few weeks practice, the fourteen-year old Bottesini learned to play the bass well enough to be admitted to the Conservatory, and the rest is history. Later, Bottesini also became very successful internationally as a conductor and composer, and in addition to various works for the double bass—works that showed off his own astonishing abilities—he wrote sacred music, orchestral music, chamber music, and a dozen operas. He died in Parma, Italy, in 1889.

Brahms, Fuchs, and Neuroscience

I'm grateful for advances in neuroscience, and for many reasons glad that every day we know more about how the brain works. But for all the studies of left brains, right brains, and networks of neurons, some things will remain mysteries, and there's no way around it. The composer Robert Fuchs (1847-1927) was a contemporary of Johannes Brahms (1833-1897). Fuchs was famous as a teacher—at the Vienna Conservatory his students included Gustav Mahler, George Enescu, and Jean Sibelius, to name just a few—and he was known and admired throughout Europe for his own compositions. Like Brahms, he wrote symphonies, choral works, organ and piano pieces, and a vast catalogue of chamber music. But have you ever heard any of this music? I'd be more than a little surprised. But I'll bet you've heard plenty of Brahms. Robert Fuchs and Johannes Brahms: one forgotten, one immortal. What did the one have that the other didn't? That's a question that neuroscience will never be able to answer.

Brahms and Tchaikovsky

Peter Ilyich Tchaikovsky (1840-1893) once referred to Johannes Brahms as a "pot-bellied boozer." He also described him as "a self-inflated mediocrity," and said that in his music Brahms had "great pretensions to profundity," but that he "never expresses anything, or, when he does, never expresses it fully." The lack of professional admiration, I'm afraid, was entirely mutual. As one historian put it, Brahms found Tchaikovsky's music "shallow and self-indulgent," and didn't even take Tchaikovsky seriously enough to consider him a rival. The two men met at least a couple of times, and once even had occasion to attend a dinner together, in Leipzig. But although the composers were outwardly cordial, it was apparently clear to all that there was no love lost between them. Brahms was a bit older—he was born in 1833 and Tchaikovsky in 1840. Strangely enough they shared a birthday, May 7, but I suspect they never sent each other birthday cards.

Johann Christian Cannabich

Johann Christian Cannabich was born in Mannheim, Germany, in 1731, and died in 1798. What's that? You've never heard of Cannabich? Well, if you'd been a music lover anywhere in Europe in the 18th century, you certainly would have. He was a violinist and a composer. He composed around seventy symphonies and 23 ballets, among other pieces, and he was the concertmaster and director of the greatest orchestra in the world, the court orchestra in Mannheim. Mozart knew Cannabich very well and knew his music, and even dedicated one of his own piano sonatas to Cannabich's daughter. Mozart gave piano lessons to the daughter, Rosina, and some say he fell in love with her along the way. The music that Cannabich wrote for the Mannheim orchestra has not exactly proved timeless, but it was very important at the time, and it influenced many later composers, including Mozart. And the important place that the Mannheim orchestra itself holds in the history of classical music is due in no small measure to the skills of Cannabich. Mozart called Johann Christian Cannabich "the best director I have ever seen."

Emmanuel Chabrier

Emmanuel Chabrier is another of those musicians who were at the center of the musical and cultural lives of their countries and their times, but whose own creative contributions have largely faded from view. Other than *España* ("Rhapsody for Orchestra") and a number of songs for voice and piano, most of Chabrier's works are likely to be unfamiliar to today's listeners, especially outside France. And yet Chabrier's circle of friends included Monet, Manet, Fauré, Chausson, Degas, and Emile Zola, just to name a few, and his music was known and admired by virtually every important composer of his day, including Mahler, Stravinsky, and Ravel. Francis Poulenc wrote that Chabrier's music had opened up a harmonic universe for him, and Ravel once said that the opening of one of Chabrier's operas had changed the course of harmony in France.

George Whitefield Chadwick

The composer George Whitefield Chadwick was born in Lowell, Massachusetts, in 1854, and died in 1931. Chadwick is in that category of composers who are generally considered "important," but whose music isn't terribly well known. He wrote a great quantity of music, including symphonies, operas, string quartets, and choral music, some of which has been revived and rediscovered. But Chadwick remains less well known today for what he wrote than for what he was, which was that rare breed, an accomplished late-19th-century *American* composer of classical music. Along with Amy Beach, Arthur Foote, Edward MacDowell, John Knowles Paine, and Horatio Parker, Chadwick was one of a group of composers known as the Boston Six. And if there was no genius of the rank of Tchaikovsky or Debussy among that group, the Boston Six were fine composers all, and they proved beyond a doubt that it was time to take American composers seriously.

Ernest Chausson

As a young man, Ernest Chausson (1855-1899) studied law and was admitted to the bar. Music, however, was his great love, and instead of practicing law, he enrolled at the Paris Conservatory, where he studied with Jules Massenet and César Franck. Chausson's family was fairly wealthy, and Chausson himself was comfortable enough financially that he never actually had to make a living as a composer. Yet he was quite prolific. He wrote many songs and other vocal works, including Chanson *perpétuelle* ("Everlasting Song") and *Poème de l'amour et de la mer* ("Poem of Love and the Sea"), both of which are for voice and orchestra; an opera, *Le roi Arthus* ("King Arthur"); a piano trio, piano quartet, works for solo piano, and an unfinished string quartet. His most famous work is undoubtedly his *Poème*, for violin and orchestra. It's hard to imagine that he wouldn't have left many more fine works, but at the age of forty-four, Ernest Chausson died when he crashed his bicycle into a brick wall.

Muzio Clementi

If you've ever taken piano lessons for more than a year or two, you've probably come across the piano sonatas of Muzio Clementi. You may even have worked on his etudes, the well known *Gradus ad Parnassum*, or "Steps to Parnassus." Clementi was born in Rome in 1752, and during his lifetime, which overlapped the lives of Haydn, Mozart, and Beethoven, he was one of the most famous musicians in the world, celebrated as a pianist and teacher of pianists, but also extremely successful as a manufacturer of pianos, and as a music publisher. As a matter of fact, he was Beethoven's exclusive publisher in England. And Beethoven was one of Clementi's greatest admirers. Beethoven's student Anton Schindler once wrote that Beethoven had "the greatest admiration for [Clementi's] sonatas, considering them the most beautiful, the most pianistic of works." After concert tours all over Europe, Clementi lived most of his adult life in England. He died in 1832, and he was buried at Westminster Abbey.

Lorenzo da Ponte

It's hard to imagine Mozart walking down Broadway, in New York City. But Lorenzo da Ponte, who wrote the words that Mozart set to music in his operas *Don Giovanni*, *The Marriage of Figaro*, and *Così fan tutte*, certainly did walk down Broadway, and he died a New Yorker. That's right. It's an amazing story, and here are the bare bones, telegraph style: Da Ponte was born in Venice; Jewish, but converted to Catholicism, and became a priest; kicked out of Venice when he had two children with his mistress; wound up in Vienna; ran out of money; moved to London with a different woman, with whom he had four more children; moved to America, opened a grocery store in Sunbury, Pennsylvania; moved to New York, opened a bookstore; became the first professor of Italian literature at Columbia University, also the first Roman Catholic priest to be appointed to the faculty, but also the first Columbia faculty member to be born Jewish. Believe me, there's more, and the full story is even more fascinating.

Claude Debussy the Pianist

Many great composers have also been terrific pianists, genuine virtuosos who in addition to composing led successful careers as performers. One gifted composer/pianist who did *not* have a big performing career was Claude Debussy (1862-1918). He did often perform his own works, but he tended to get nervous, and he didn't enjoy playing in public. And yet by all accounts Debussy was a wonderful pianist, especially noted for his beautiful "touch" at the keyboard. "How could one forget his suppleness, the caress of his touch?" wrote the famous French pianist Marguerite Long, a contemporary of Debussy. "While floating over the keys with a curiously penetrating gentleness, he could achieve an extraordinary power of expression." Alfredo Casella, another great pianist and Debussy contemporary, wrote, "He made the impression of playing directly on the strings of the instrument with no intermediate mechanism; the effect was a miracle of poetry."

Debussy the Writer

Like many other famous composers, Claude Debussy was also a wonderful writer. He wrote countless articles of music criticism, and his writing was clever, funny, insightful, highly opinionated, and often wickedly caustic. He wrote some of his articles under the pseudonym Monsieur Croche, which in French means "Mr. Eighth Note," but whether writing as Monsieur Croche or himself, he was never shy about saying what he thought. One of his most famous sentences, for example, concerns Richard Wagner. "The music of Wagner," wrote Debussy, "was a beautiful sunset that people mistook for a dawn." And there's no question that Debussy admired Beethoven's genius, but in a comment about a performance of Beethoven's song "Adelaïde"—a song that I have to confess is one of my personal favorites—Debussy wrote, "I think that the old master had forgotten to burn this song, and that we have to place the blame for this exhumation on the backs of overly greedy heirs."

Is This About Debussy?

Here are a few words that one great composer wrote about another, and I wonder if you'll be able to guess who was writing about whom. "One finds again [in this piece] an almost pure form of this 'musical arabesque'…[but] in taking up the arabesque again he rendered it more supple, more fluid, and, despite the strict discipline that the great master imposed on Beauty, [the arabesque] was propelled with a free fancy, always fresh, that astonishes us to this day." "He laughed off harmonic formulas, that's for sure. He preferred the free play of sonorities whose curves… produced an unexpected of flowering that imbued even the least of his innumerable works with an imperishable beauty." Did the name Claude Debussy happen to occur to you? Well, you were right to think of him. But that wasn't a description of Debussy's music. Those were the words of Claude Debussy, writing about the music of Johann Sebastian Bach.

Debussy and Ravel

Claude Debussy and Maurice Ravel were roughly contemporaries, and as two of the greatest figures in late 19th and early 20th-century French music, they tend to be linked in people's minds. But although they had similar training and came under many of the same influences, their musical styles and techniques were really quite different. And each admired the other's talents, but that didn't stop either one of them from criticizing what he saw as the other's weaknesses. Debussy was perhaps harder on Ravel than the other way around, because although Ravel complained about certain aspects of Debussy's writing for the orchestra and for the piano, he also called Debussy "the most phenomenal genius in the history of French music." And according to one interviewer Ravel once said that "his dearest wish would be to die gently lulled in the tender and voluptuous embrace of Claude Debussy's *Prelude to the Afternoon of a Faun.*"

Maurice Duruflé

The French composer Maurice Duruflé (1902–1986) belongs to two interesting categories. One is the category of composers who were better known during their lifetimes for something other than composing, and the other is the category of composers whose lasting reputations are based on just one piece. Duruflé was one of the most famous of 20th-century French organists, and it was for his organ playing that he was best known during his lifetime. He spent his entire professional career as a church organist in Paris, but he also toured as an organ virtuoso throughout Europe and the United States. As a composer he was extremely self-critical, and his entire output consists of only about 15 pieces. Several of his organ works are very well regarded, at least among organists, and he wrote a lovely trio for flute, viola, and piano. But it is with his *Requiem*, a work that many consider one of the most beautiful choral works of the 20th century, that Duruflé achieved musical immortality.

Dvořák and Spirituals

The composer Ernest Bloch once wrote that it's only by plunging one's roots to the depths of one's own people that one finds the common ground of all people. Antonin Dvořák (1841-1904) expressed a similar sentiment, and here's the advice that he gave to American composers at the beginning of the 20th century, after he had been introduced to Negro spirituals (a term that African-American scholars still use): "I am now satisfied that the future music of this country must be founded upon what are called the negro melodies. They are the songs of America and your composers must turn to them. In the negro melodies…I discover all that is needed for a great and noble school of music. They are pathetic, tender, passionate, melancholy, solemn, religious, bold, merry, gay, gracious or what you will. It is music that suits itself to any mood or purpose. There is nothing in the whole range of composition that cannot find a thematic source here."

Dvořák, Tchaikovsky, and Melody

Already during their lifetimes, Antonin Dvořák and Peter Ilyich Tchaikovsky were among the most famous composers in the world. Their music is extremely sophisticated, the product of highly skilled artists, and their beautiful melodies have always been especially beloved. Some critics, though, have pooh-poohed Dvořák and Tchaikovsky as being "just" melodists. Well. First of all, Dvořák and Tchaikovsky both labored long and hard at their compositions. It turns out it's not so easy to write melodies, especially beautiful, immortal melodies. Those critics should try it some time. And to put things in perspective, here are the words of the composer Hans Gàl: "Civilized man, living in a world riddled with artificiality, is in danger of forgetting primary phenomena. In our day it seems necessary to point out that melody is such a primary phenomenon, and that there has never been a period in history when melody was not the essence of what people considered to be music."

Gabriel Fauré

Gabriel Fauré (1845-1924) is often referred to as one of the greatest French composers of the late nineteenth and early twentieth centuries. But I wonder if that description goes far enough. It's certainly true that Fauré's contributions to French music—especially in the areas of chamber music, piano music, and music for the voice—are outstanding. But they're outstanding because they're wonderful music, not because they're French. It's all very well to be aware of a composer's nationality and of the specific cultural forces that have influenced him, but sometimes the influence goes in the other direction. Perhaps we should consider this: that it may be more accurate, instead of saying that Fauré sounds French, to say that French music of the late nineteenth and early twentieth centuries sounds like Fauré. In any case, if it were up to me I would simply say that Fauré deserves recognition as one of the greatest composers of that era, period.

Vincenzo Galilei

The man usually referred to simply as Galileo, whose full name was Galileo Galilei, was a pivotal figure in the history of science. What may surprise you is that Galileo's father, *Vincenzo* Galilei, born in Italy in 1520, was a pivotal figure in the history of Western music. The elder Galilei was a lutenist, singer, and composer, but most importantly he was a theorist. In a book called *Dialogue of Ancient and Modern Music*, published in 1581, he laid out the theory of what came to be known as *monody*, the style of music that features a solo vocal line with instrumental accompaniment. Galilei argued that polyphony, the dominant style of the Renaissance, lacked dramatic clarity because of its multiple simultaneous voices. Monody was meant to imitate what some scholars thought to be the style of music of the ancient Greek dramas, and it was the rise of monody—championed by Galilei—that led directly to the invention of opera. Vincenzo Galilei died in Florence in 1591.

Philippe Gaubert

Here's a name you almost certainly know if you're a flutist but probably don't if you're not: Philippe Gaubert. And yet Philippe Gaubert (1879-1941) was one of the most famous and important French musicians of the first half of the twentieth century. As a teenager in the 1890s, Gaubert studied the flute at the Paris Conservatory with the great French flutist Paul Taffanel, and eventually the signature style of the legendary teacher and his brilliant pupil became known as "the French method." Taffanel and Gaubert collaborated on a teaching text called *Méthode Complète de Flûte*, "Complete Flute Method," usually called simply "Taffanel/Gaubert" by the countless flutists all over the world who still use it. Gaubert himself, though, didn't just stick to the flute. He became a fine composer and a distinguished conductor, eventually rising to the exalted and powerful position of director of the Paris Opera. Philippe Gaubert—a musician famous in *his* time, known mainly to specialists in ours.

Great and Good (and Ginastera)

I was looking not long ago at a list of composers who were born on April 11. One birthday name I recognized immediately: Alberto Ginastera. Ginastera (1916-1983) wrote works in virtually every major genre, and he was among the most important Argentinian composers of the twentieth century. But I was struck by the fact that of the twenty-three other names on the birthday list, I knew none. And yet during their lifetimes some of these composers were undoubtedly quite well known, wrote some pretty good music, made good livings, and shared the pleasure of hearing their works played by excellent musicians. Were they failures? Only if they themselves thought they were. Where, after all, is it written that being good is bad, and that only greatness is good?

Ferd Grofé

These days, the one piece by the American composer Ferd Grofé (1892-1972) that many concertgoers still know is the composer's *Grand Canyon Suite*, with its familiar "On the Trail" section. But perhaps I should say that the *Grand Canyon Suite* is the only piece by Grofé that people *think* they know. Grofé started his career as a violist with the Los Angeles Symphony, but his great love was jazz piano, and while still in his twenties he landed a job as pianist and arranger with the famous Paul Whiteman Band. It was for Whiteman that Grofé wrote the music that will guarantee his immortality: his arrangement for jazz band of George Gershwin's *Rhapsody in Blue*. And actually Grofé's immortality is doubly guaranteed, because he also wrote the wonderful orchestral arrangement of *Rhapsody in Blue* that concertgoers all over the world know and love.

Franz Anton Hoffmeister

The Viennese composer Franz Anton Hoffmeister (1754-1812) is yet another example of a composer who was extremely well known and well regarded in his day, but very little known in ours. He wrote at least nine operas, more than sixty symphonies, dozens of pieces for the flute, and hundreds of chamber music pieces of various kinds. He also wrote a viola concerto, and a set of demanding études for viola, études that have provided me countless hours of combined pleasure and frustration. Hoffmeister was also a very important publisher of music, particularly famous for publishing the works of his good friend Mozart, as well as the works of Bach, Haydn, and Beethoven. Most of what Hoffmeister himself wrote never gets played anymore, which is perhaps not surprising, but which in a way is too bad, because much of his music is well written, fun to play, and quite charming. Not every piece needs to be a masterpiece, after all, to be worth our while. Sometimes *delightful* is enough.

Gustav Holst

The English composer Gustav Holst (1874-1934) was remarkably prolific: he wrote eight operas, four ballets, dozens of choral works and songs, many large works for orchestra and for band, concertos, chamber music pieces, and works for solo piano. To today's audiences, though, Holst is primarily known for just one of those many works, his orchestral suite called *The Planets*. Now I suppose it's much better to be remembered for one work than for nothing at all, and *The Planets* remains spectacularly popular. Holst also borrowed his own tune, from the "Jupiter" section of *The Planets*, to fashion a hymn called "I Vow to Thee, My Country," and that hymn has become beloved in its own right all over the world.

Erich Wolfgang Korngold

Erich Wolfgang Korngold was born in 1897. When he was ten years old, he composed a cantata. When he was eleven he wrote a ballet. At twelve he wrote a stunning piano trio, and at thirteen he wrote a piano sonata that the famous virtuoso Artur Schnabel performed all over Europe. Gustav Mahler called the young Korngold a genius, and Richard Strauss wrote that "one's first reactions to the fact that these compositions are by an adolescent boy are those of awe and fear." Korngold's greatest fame came after he escaped to America from Vienna in the 1930s and became one of the most brilliant composers in the history of film music. He wrote the scores for eighteen movies and won two Academy Awards, but in the mid-1940s he retired from film composing and rededicated himself to writing for the concert hall. Perhaps his best-known concert work is his violin concerto, which was premiered in 1947 by no less a figure than Jascha Heifetz, and which is still played all over the world. Korngold died in Los Angeles in 1957.

Joseph Lanner

Don Drysdale was a great pitcher for the Los Angeles Dodgers in the 1950s and 60s, but you don't usually hear his name mentioned without hearing the name of another, and even greater Dodger pitcher of the same era, Sandy Koufax. Well, Joseph Lanner (1801-1843) was a hugely popular and important composer and orchestra leader in Vienna in the 1820s and 30s, one of the first composers to create a refined version of the Viennese waltz and bring it into the dance hall. But you won't often hear Lanner's name without also hearing the name Johann Strauss. Strauss—that's Johann Strauss *Senior*—started out as a kind of assistant to Lanner, but the two split, and they became friendly rivals, each with his own set of passionate fans. Eventually Strauss became an international touring sensation and much more famous than his former boss, who never left Vienna, and who had the misfortune to die young.

Guillaume Lekeu

We know that Mozart, Schubert, and Mendelssohn all died too young: Mozart at thirty-five, Schubert at thirty-one, Mendelssohn at thirty-eight. But all three left us many masterpieces, and luckily we can concentrate on what was, rather than on what might have been. The Belgian composer Guillaume Lekeu was just twenty-two when he wrote a violin sonata for his countryman Eugène Ysaÿe, and that sonata became a favorite of many of the 20th century's greatest violinists. Lekeu composed a number of other chamber works, most when he was a teenager, and he left behind two movements of a spectacularly beautiful piano quartet. He didn't live to write the third movement. Born on January 20, 1870, Lekeu died of typhoid fever one day after his twenty-fourth birthday, on January 21, 1894. And we'll always have to wonder what might have been.

Charles Martin Loeffler

I'm always intrigued by the stories of musicians who were famous and important in their own time but whose reputations have at some point dipped or dimmed or even disappeared, sometimes for no obvious reason. Are you familiar with the music of Charles Martin Loeffler? Loeffler was born in Germany in 1861, and in 1881 he emigrated to America, where he had a distinguished career as both a violinist and composer. He was co-concertmaster of the Boston Symphony Orchestra, and the Boston Symphony was just one of the orchestras that often performed his compositions. John Singer Sargent painted his portrait, and Ferruccio Busoni and Gabriel Fauré both dedicated pieces to him. I've played two of Loeffler's works, his *Two Rhapsodies* for oboe, viola, and piano, and his *Four Poems* for mezzo-soprano, viola, and piano, and they're both lovely. And as I discover more of his works I find myself wondering if it's just a matter of time before his time comes again. Loeffler died in Massachusetts in 1935.

Felix Mendelssohn

Musical child prodigies have always fascinated the public. Far more rare than the child prodigy performer, though, is the child prodigy composer. The first name that comes to many people's minds when they think of child composers is Mozart, and it's true that Mozart started writing music at the age of four or five. But of all Mozart's great pieces, very few were written before his twentieth birthday. Felix Mendelssohn, on the other hand, composed masterpieces when he was fifteen, sixteen, and seventeen, pieces that far surpass anything Mozart wrote when *he* was a teenager. Mendelssohn was just sixteen, for example, when he wrote his famous Octet for strings, and seventeen when he wrote the *Overture to A Midsummer Night's Dream*. It's true that adolescents feel things very deeply and intensely, but it remains astonishing that a teenage boy could write music that will move men and women and stir their souls for as long as music is played. I should also mention that, while still a teenager, Mendelssohn had translated major Latin works into German and had become an accomplished artist in pencil and watercolor. He was a brilliant pianist and excellent violinist and violist, and he revolutionized orchestral conducting. In addition to German and Latin, he spoke English and Italian and made German translations from those languages as well as from ancient Greek, and by all accounts he was just a terrifically nice guy. Felix Mendelssohn—a miraculous human being. He was born in Hamburg, Germany, on February 3, 1809, and died in Leipzig on November 4, 1847.

Ernest John Moeran

Many musical works, and many composers, fall into obscurity for very good reasons. My colleagues and I have been known to joke about pieces we call "justly neglected." It's a particular pleasure, then, to discover the truly unjustly neglected composer or piece. I suppose my own ignorance of 20th-century English music is to blame, but until recently I had never heard of a composer named Ernest John Moeran. But then I saw his name on a list of English composers, and I decided to investigate. Moeran was born in 1894 and died in 1950, and he wrote songs, piano pieces, chamber music, concertos, symphonies, and choral works. I've heard a recording of his String Trio, and I think it's a piece that deserves to be heard more often. Many of Moeran's other works have also been recorded, it turns out, and I'm looking forward to additional delightful discoveries.

Mozart's Optimism

It's hard to find a classical music lover who doesn't love the music of Mozart. It's when we try to describe *why* we love Mozart that things can get complicated. We're describing something indisputably real, our love of Mozart, but unless we stick to strictly technical analyses, we have to use words that will necessarily be both subjective and metaphorical. My own words? I keep coming back to two: humanity and optimism. What I somehow hear in Mozart, whether in his operas or his instrumental works, is both a deep understanding of humanity and a deep affection for humanity, for human beings with all their foibles and frailties. I also hear a kind of fundamental optimism. Not a vision of Utopia, or of Triumph and Transcendence, but the simple optimism that says that it's important to be joyful when we can; to know that things often really do turn out all right; and to remember that all in all it's wonderful to be alive.

Playing Mozart

I know I don't have to tell you how wonderful Mozart's music is to listen to, but if you're not a musician yourself you may find it interesting to know that Mozart's music is also wonderful to play. And it's not that it's *easy* to play. It's usually pretty hard, and sometimes very hard. But it's never stupidly or needlessly hard. With enough practice it's always playable, and it's always satisfying to play. Mozart was a performer himself, and he knew what gave performers pleasure. A violist colleague of mine once said that he'd enjoy playing Mozart string quartets even with soap on his bow—making no sound, in other words—just for the pleasure of the physical movements. And in 1901, Claude Debussy wrote a concert review in which he said, "Next Monsieur Pugno played a concerto by Mozart that can't be played badly, it being so well written for the piano."

Mozart – What the Letters Show

If you've seen the movie *Amadeus*, or the play it was based on, you may have gotten the impression that Wolfgang Amadeus Mozart was some sort of giggling idiot who just happened to be really good at writing music. Nothing could be further from the truth. Read a collection of Mozart's letters and you discover a person who is serious, articulate, witty, and perceptive; someone who writes beautifully and can make jokes—sometimes very dirty jokes, it's true—in at least three different languages. Mozart's native language was German, but he spoke Italian and French quite well, and his Latin was apparently excellent. The letters also show that Mozart was a keen and skilled observer of human nature, which should come as no surprise if we think about the wonderful and complex characters in his operas. And he was also an expert, and a very funny one, when it came to puncturing pretensions, especially when the pretensions he was puncturing belonged to a person of exalted social status.

Mozart's Don Giovanni – Beauty, Falsehood, and Genius

One of the reasons Mozart's operas seem so profound to us is that they're so true to life, and perhaps especially true to life's ironies and contradictions. Take the character of Don Giovanni. He's introduced to us having committed a sexual assault, which he follows by killing someone. But Mozart doesn't make him a cartoon villain, he does the opposite: he makes him appealing—he gives him beautiful music to sing. But here's what's so fascinating, and such a stroke of genius on Mozart's part: every gorgeous note Don Giovanni sings is a lie. Consider the aria *Deh vieni alla finestra, o mio tesoro* ("Come to the window, O my treasure"), which Don Giovanni sings beneath the window of Donna Elvira. It's a serenade, a love song, and a very beautiful one. And it's a fake. Don Giovanni doesn't love Donna Elvira; he's just trying to seduce her. Mozart uses beautiful music to show the *danger* of beauty; to show that beauty can be false, and even that music itself can lie. And at the same time he shows that people sometimes *want* to be lied to, depending on how it's done and by whom. It would have been so much easier to make Don Giovanni a sort of barking bad guy and singer of nasty songs. But Mozart's way is much more profound. It's not just true to life, it's true to the painful complexities of life.

Mesmer and Mozart

If you explore the history of psychotherapy, you'll come upon the name Franz Anton Mesmer. Mesmer was born in Germany in 1734, and it was Mesmer who invented the term "animal magnetism," which is what he called the mysterious force, or fluid, that flowed through his own body and that he could redirect for therapeutic purposes. Before you laugh, you should know that Mesmer had many therapeutic successes and many disciples, and for a period in his life he was rich and famous. And it's from Mesmer's name that we get the word "mesmerize." What does this have to do with music? Well, in 1767 Mesmer moved to a magnificent estate in Vienna, and among the guests he entertained there were the composers Gluck and Haydn. Leopold Mozart and his family were frequent guests, too, and when Leopold's 12-year-old son, Wolfgang, wrote an opera called *Bastien und Bastienne*, the premiere took place in Dr. Mesmer's private theater. Mozart must eventually have lost whatever admiration he may once have had for Mesmer, however, because in his opera *Così fan tutte* he makes merciless fun of Mesmer and his "magnetic stone."

Mozart Flute Quartets

In a famous letter to his father, Mozart once wrote, "you know I become quite powerless whenever I am obliged to write for an instrument I cannot bear." He was talking about the flute, and the occasion of the letter was a commission Mozart had received to write several flute concertos and quartets for flute and strings. In fairness to Mozart, neither the flutes nor the flutists of his day were overly reliable, but it's also possible that Mozart had just been procrastinating, and was inventing an excuse to give his father. In any case, the works he wrote for flute, including four flute quartets and two concertos—one of which, it's true, started life as an oboe concerto—are all among the jewels of the flute repertoire. Mozart was still Mozart, after all, and in the same letter to his father he also wrote, "a composition goes into the world, and naturally I do not want to have reason to be ashamed of my name on the title page."

About Mozart

A few interesting comments about Mozart...

From Tchaikovsky: "I not only love Mozart—I worship him... He gave the first impulse to my musical powers and made me love music more than anything else in the world."

From George Bernard Shaw: "In the subtleties of dramatic instrumentation, Mozart was the greatest master of them all."

From pianist Artur Schnabel: "The sonatas of Mozart are unique. They are too easy for children and too difficult for artists."

From Rossini: "I take [Beethoven] twice a week, Haydn four times, and Mozart every day."

And from the early 19th-century critic Thomas Love Peacock: "There is nothing perfect in this world except Mozart's music."

Mozart's Death

On December 5, 1791, Wolfgang Amadeus Mozart died. He was thirty-five years old. He died at home in Vienna, with his wife, Constanze, by his bedside. Over the years there have been various theories and rumors about what killed Mozart, including the rumor that he was poisoned by his musical rival Antonio Salieri. This rumor survived for many reasons, including contemporary accounts that Mozart himself felt that he had somehow been poisoned. Most experts today, however, feel that it was most likely rheumatic fever that killed Mozart, and it wasn't a pretty death. In the composer's final days, his body swelled all over to the point that he could barely move, and he suffered other miseries, the details of which are even more gruesome. Up until the end, though, Mozart continued to work. Two months before his death, already sick, he conducted the premiere of his opera *The Magic Flute*, and just weeks before he died he composed his great Clarinet Concerto. His final work, left unfinished, was a *Requiem*, and the story we're told is that Mozart knew he was writing it for himself.

Isaac Nathan

Isaac Nathan was born in Canterbury, England in 1790. He was Jewish, and he originally trained for life in the synagogue, as a cantor. Early on though, he switched paths and became, among other things, a voice teacher and composer. In London he wrote the music for several successful musical comedies, but his greatest success came as the composer of a collection of songs called "Hebrew Melodies." Nathan's music was largely based on old Jewish songs and synagogue tunes, but the poems for the songs were provided by none other than Lord Byron. The "Hebrew Melodies" were first published in 1815 and were extremely popular, selling thousands of copies (the composer Max Bruch borrowed one of the songs in the collection for the second theme of his *Kol Nidrei* for cello and orchestra), but Nathan later ran into financial troubles and moved to Australia. He became an important figure in the musical history of Australia, but on January 15, 1864, Isaac Nathan also became the first person in Australia ever to be run over and killed by a horse-drawn tram.

David Popper

Have you ever heard of a composer named David Popper? If you're not a cellist, your answer is very likely, "Nope." But if you *are* a cellist, your answer is, "Well of course." There are some composers whose reputations rest almost entirely on their works for one instrument, and who, although they may not have been composers of the first rank, wrote brilliantly for that one instrument. Popper, who was born in Prague, in 1843, and who died in 1913, is a perfect example. He was a virtuoso cellist himself, and in his compositions he stretched the limits of cello playing beyond where they'd ever been. Was he a great composer? Well, no, but virtually all the world's cellists, even if they can't actually play the pieces themselves, are familiar with such David Popper works as "Tarantella," "Dance of the Elves," and "Spinning Song." And cello students everywhere have struggled with Popper's *High School of Cello Playing*, a book of études that's a kind of Mount Everest of cello technique.

Francis Poulenc

The image of the starving artist may be a romantic one, but it turns out that poverty has not always been a necessary condition for writing great music. Sometimes, great music has gone along with great wealth. Felix Mendelssohn, for one, came from a very wealthy family, and during his lifetime Johannes Brahms made more money than he could ever use. Closer to our own time, the best example of a wealthy genius may have been the French composer Francis Poulenc (1899-1963). Poulenc was the grandson of the founder of the firm that became Rhône-Poulenc, a giant chemical and pharmaceutical manufacturer, and he wouldn't have had to work a day in his life if he hadn't wanted to. But work he did. He toured for many years as a professional pianist, and he composed an immense body of work in a wide variety of musical forms: brilliant and delightful songs and chamber music pieces; sacred music, including a beautiful *Gloria* for soprano, chorus, and orchestra; a ballet, *Les Biches*; and three operas, including his masterpiece, *Dialogues of the Carmelites*. In his personal life, Poulenc was famously fun-loving and charming, but he also suffered from periods of deep depression. In his thirties he experienced a profound religious awakening, and it was apparently a source of great strength for him.

Sergei Prokofiev

Sergei Prokofiev (1891-1953) was a giant of 20th-century composition. He wrote wonderful symphonies, operas, ballets, concertos, piano sonatas, and chamber music pieces, in addition to the perennial children's favorite *Peter and the Wolf*. Some things you may not know: Prokofiev visited the United States a number of times, and his concerts here were extremely successful. His opera *The Love for Three Oranges* was premiered in Chicago, and he met his first wife, the soprano Lina Llubera, in New York City. The Prokofievs lived in Paris in the 1920s and 30s, but they later returned to the Soviet Union, where I'm afraid their marriage fell apart. For some reason, Lina was later arrested, and she spent eight years in a Soviet gulag. Prokofiev died a world-famous composer, but his death was overshadowed in the newspapers by the death of another man who died the same day: Josef Stalin.

Giacomo Puccini

Giacomo Puccini was born in 1858, and he died in 1924. Even a partial list of Puccini's works reads like an "Opera's Greatest Hits" list: *La Bohème, Tosca, Madama Butterfly, Manon Lescaut, Turandot.* Over the last hundred years these operas have been performed thousands of times all over the world, and they've served as showcases for the greatest singers of every generation. Puccini came from a long line of famous Italian church musicians, and at first he was expected to follow in their footsteps. But at the age of 17 he attended a performance of Giuseppe Verdi's *Aida,* and it changed his life. Puccini's first great success came in 1893, with *Manon Lescaut,* and after seeing just that one Puccini opera George Bernard Shaw wrote, "Puccini looks to me more like the heir of Verdi than any of his rivals." And he was right.

Johann Joachim Quantz

If you're not a flutist or Baroque music specialist, the name Johann Joachim Quantz (1697-1793) may not mean much to you. But if you are, you know that Quantz was probably the most celebrated flutist, and flute composer, of the Baroque era. He wrote hundreds of flute sonatas and concertos, and he also *made* flutes, and devised improvements in the instrument so that it played more reliably in tune. Quantz is also the author of a very famous book, *Versuch einer Anweisung die Flöte traversiere zu spielen,* or, in English, *Playing the Flute*—but the book is really about much more than just playing the flute, and it remains a very important reference work for the study of Baroque performance practice. Among his other accomplishments, Quantz gained great fame as the flute teacher and composer for Frederick the Great of Prussia, and one of the flutes that Quantz made for Frederick now sits in a beautiful porcelain box in the instrument collection of the Library of Congress, in Washington, DC.

Sergei Rachmaninoff

Sergei Rachmaninoff (1873-1943) was an example of one of the great "types" in the history of classical music: the virtuoso performer who was also an important composer. And indeed he was one of the supreme examples of this type, because both his performing and his composing activities were on the highest level. During his time, in fact, Rachmaninoff was considered by many to be nothing less than the greatest pianist in the world, and if you have the opportunity to sample some of the many Rachmaninoff recordings, I think you'll see why. Unlike many composers who eventually curtailed their performing careers, Rachmaninoff kept up a very busy—actually a punishingly busy—concert schedule. But his gifts were such that despite such a schedule, and despite struggles with serious emotional problems, Rachmaninoff managed to compose works that will be played and sung for as long as people are still playing and singing.

Maurice Ravel – Part 1

A famous music critic once referred to the French composer Maurice Ravel (1875-1937) as "this most conscious, most naturally artificial of composers." Ravel himself claimed that he wasn't seeking "profundity" in the music he wrote, he was merely seeking *perfection*—some sort of technical perfection in composition, as he defined it, with "absolute beauty" as the guidepost and goal. But here's the problem: I'm not sure we should completely believe him. He once said, "In my opinion the *joie de vivre* expressed in dance goes much deeper than the puritanism of César Franck." Ravel borrowed dance rhythms from his own country and from Spain, Austria, and America (by way of jazz), and I think his brilliant exploitation of those rhythms shows that in order to achieve depth, you don't always have to dig.

Maurice Ravel – Part 2

It's one of the hallmarks of great composers that they're not limited by the practices of their times. Their imaginations are enriched, but not hemmed in, by the traditions they inherit, and they tend to push boundaries. Maurice Ravel was certainly a composer who pushed boundaries, including the technical boundaries that musicians faced when performing his music. The story goes that when Ravel was writing his Sonata for Violin and Cello, he invited the virtuoso cellist André Lévy, a good friend of his, to have a look at the cello part. Ravel asked Lévy if he thought it would be possible to play the cello part as written. Lévy took a good long look and said, "Well, Maurice, it's very difficult." To which Ravel replied, "I didn't ask whether it was difficult, I asked whether it was possible." I love that story for what it tells us about Ravel, about both his humility and his self-confidence, but also for how it reminds us of the courage and daring of all great creative artists.

Alexander Reinagle – and George Washington

When you think of George Washington, do you automatically think of...Alexander Reinagle? Well, maybe not, but if you did you'd be within your rights. I'll explain. Reinagle was a keyboard player and composer who was born in England in 1756 but who came to America in 1786, landing first in New York and then moving to Philadelphia. He was a close friend of C. P. E. Bach (a son of J. S. Bach, and an important composer in his own right), and is said to have introduced Philadelphia to the music of Haydn and Mozart. And one of his greatest admirers, it turns out, was none other than George Washington. Washington once wrote that he himself could "neither sing...nor raise a single note of any instrument," but that "nothing is more agreeable and ornamental, than good music." Washington apparently often listened to that good music at Alexander Reinagle's concerts, and he thought so highly of Reinagle that he engaged him to teach music to his adopted granddaughter, Nelly Custis. Reinagle died in Baltimore, in 1809.

Schubert's Popularity

In 1928, the centenary of Franz Schubert's death (he was born in 1797), one well-known critic began a celebratory essay with the ironic observation that Schubert had avoided the "indignity of too much popularity." The critic lamented the fact that at that time, i.e., well into the 20th century, much of Schubert's music remained unknown, even among musicians. Part of the problem, it must be admitted, was that people simply hadn't had the chance to hear very much of the music. Schubert was not exactly the savviest businessman or self-promoter in the history of music, and many of his works weren't published, or even publicly performed, until many years after his death. Thank goodness, then, for astute critics, and for the musicians who eventually did recognize the greatness of Schubert's music and brought virtually all of it back to life. Schubert's own life was lamentably short, and marked by poverty and illness. It seems a terribly unjust fate for someone who brought so much beauty into the world. But time passes and great music endures, and if there's such a thing as *musical* justice, in Schubert's case it's been richly served.

Schubert Symphony No. 9

In 1838, ten years after the death of Franz Schubert, the composer Robert Schumann traveled to Vienna, and while he was there he paid a visit to the graves of Schubert and Beethoven. On a whim, Schumann decided to call on Schubert's brother, Ferdinand, who was living in Vienna, and this turned out to be perhaps the most important and rewarding social call in the history of music. That's because Ferdinand showed Schumann a bunch of his brother's unpublished manuscripts, and among them was the manuscript, the long-forgotten manuscript, of Schubert's Symphony No. 9, now known as the "Great C Major" Symphony to distinguish it from Schubert's Symphony No. 6, a smaller work also in C Major. Schumann immediately recognized the unpublished symphony as a masterpiece, a work, he later wrote, that takes us far beyond "mere ordinary joy and sorrow" to "a region that we never before explored." He sent the music on to Felix Mendelssohn, who had it played by the Leipzig Gewandhaus Orchestra, and the rest is history. But imagine if Schumann hadn't made that social call…

Dmitri Shostakovich

The political views of Dmitri Shostakovich (1906-1975) have long been subjects of controversy. Was Shostakovich a loyal Communist, or was he a secret rebel who contrived time and again to encode subversive messages into his music? Well, I hate to make light of questions that for Shostakovich himself may truly have been issues of life and death, but in the long run, the answer is simple: it doesn't much matter. What matters is that Shostakovich was a brilliant composer who wrote enduring masterpieces. What he was thinking or feeling when he wrote them is anybody's guess, and most guesses will be wrong. They will be wrong because from bar to bar and note to note a composer's creative choices are musical, not political, and like creative choices in *all* the arts, they emerge from wellsprings that are deep and mysterious.

Jean Sibelius

Jean Sibelius was a fascinating man. He was born in 1865, the year the American Civil War ended, and he died in 1957, the year of Sputnik. He was prolific—he composed seven symphonies, many other orchestral works, a magnificent violin concerto, choral music, music for the stage, various chamber music works, and more than a hundred songs—but for reasons that remain mysterious, over the last thirty years of his life he wrote virtually nothing. He was the greatest of Finnish composers, but he was a Swedish Finn: his first language was Swedish, and although he spoke Finnish, Swedish was the language in which he was always most at home. Sibelius was influenced by many of the 19th-century composers who preceded him, and his Second Symphony, completed in 1902, is considered one of the last great Romantic symphonies. But Sibelius was a composer whose style was always completely personal and impossible to pigeonhole.

Louis Spohr

Sic transit gloria mundi. Thus passes worldly glory. Louis Spohr was born in Germany in 1784 and died in 1859. During his lifetime he was one of the most renowned musicians in all of Europe, famed as violinist, conductor, and composer. He wrote ten symphonies, ten operas, eighteen violin concertos, four clarinet concertos, and thirty-six string quartets, among dozens of other works, and along the way he found time to teach a couple of hundred violin students, write an influential book about violin technique, invent the violin chinrest, and pioneer the use of the baton for conducting orchestras. Some of his music is quite appealing and is still played, or has been rediscovered—Louis Spohr isn't one of those composers who has fallen into complete obscurity. But for better or for worse, the majority of his works remain unknown to modern audiences.

Georg Philipp Telemann

You could write a book about the life of the German composer Georg Philipp Telemann (1681-1767). And as it turns out, Telemann himself wrote three—three separate autobiographies. One of the things he wrote about is the time he spent in Poland in his early twenties. He became familiar with Polish and Moravian folk music during this period—he wrote that he experienced it in "all its barbaric beauty"—and he also heard the music of the Romani. But he didn't just listen: he incorporated some of the folk tunes he heard into his own music. It's funny, because we don't usually think of Telemann as a composer who was inspired by wandering folk musicians, but in one of his autobiographies, he wrote, "One can hardly believe what wonderful imaginative ideas these pipers and fiddlers have as they improvise. In only a week, a composer could be inspired for an entire lifetime."

Giuseppe Verdi

Here are the names of seven composers of Italian opera who were contemporaries of Giuseppe Verdi (1813-1901): Filippo Marchetti, Errico Petrella, Pietro Antonio Coppola, Luigi Ricci, Federico Ricci, Antonio Cagnoni, and Giovanni Pacini. Ever heard of them? Neither had I. But among them, those seven composers wrote 172 operas. So why is it that Verdi's operas have lasted, and those other 172 haven't? Why do we still know *Rigoletto, La Traviata, Il Trovatore*? Surely Verdi didn't have a monopoly on talent. The musicologist Donald Jay Grout's answer is that Verdi surpassed his contemporaries by combining rare melodic and harmonic gifts with what Grout calls "dynamic individuality" and a "ferocious energy of expression." For Verdi, in other words, musical genius and personal passion were perfectly matched. And the results were unmatched.

Antonio Vivaldi

Antonio Vivaldi was born in Venice in 1678, and at the age of twenty-five he was ordained as a priest. Early on, though, he gave up his religious duties for music, and he then became perhaps the most celebrated violin virtuoso and composer in all of Europe, with a rather colorful lifestyle that included serving as music director at an institute for orphaned girls and traveling all over the continent with his mistress. The colorful lifestyle eventually got him into trouble, and to make a very long story very short, he wound up with no job, no money, and in Vienna of all places, where he died, in 1741, and where he was buried in a pauper's grave. But his music, especially his hundreds of concertos, proved to be a treasure trove, and an important source of ideas and inspiration for many other composers, including, most notably, Johann Sebastian Bach.

William Walton

The English composer William Walton, or *Sir* William Walton (1892-1983) is famous for several important works, including *Façade*, his first big success, which is a piece for "reciter" and chamber ensemble, a cantata called *Belshazzar's Feast*, which is often considered one of the major English choral works of the twentieth century, and a violin concerto written for Jascha Heifetz. But I play the viola, and for me, Walton will always be a composer to treasure because he wrote one of the greatest of all viola concertos. He wrote it in 1929 for the English violist Lionel Tertis, and although Tertis later played the piece, he declined the premiere. The first performance was played instead by Paul Hindemith, a major composer in his own right and also a very accomplished violist. Walton modeled his concerto— modeled it very closely—on the Violin Concerto No. 1 of Sergei Prokofiev (see "How I Won Ten Dollars From Leonard Bernstein," above), but he managed nonetheless to compose a compellingly personal and brilliant work.

What (Who) Will Last?

Perhaps you've thought about this: Bach and Mozart died over two hundred years ago; is there anybody alive today whose music will be played two hundred years from *now*? It's a tricky question. There are contemporary composers whose music I like and admire, but I certainly wouldn't bet my life on predicting their immortality. When it comes to the great composers of the past, we're lucky: history has done the winnowing for us. You may be able to quickly tick off your fifteen favorite composers from the Baroque, Classical, and Romantic eras, but over the span of those eras there were literally hundreds of people writing music, and most of those people have been completely forgotten. Many of them were very accomplished. They were undoubtedly highly respected and admired, and they enriched the lives of their contemporaries. But history isn't always generous. And when it comes to today's composers, I'm afraid none of us will still be around to see who makes the cut.

III. PERFORMERS AND PERFORMING

Paradox of Integrity

Musicians, like actors, have to deal with something a drama teacher once called the "paradox of integrity." On the one hand, you have to be completely "in character" when you're performing: identified with the music, and moved yourself in order to make the music moving for others. At literally the same time, however, you have to remain completely conscious of all necessary musical details, starting with what the notes are and how you plan to play them or sing them for optimal expression and effect. But is this really a paradox? I don't think so. I think it's virtually the definition of human nature, of our ability to manage simultaneous processes and simultaneous levels of awareness. And is it so different from what we do when we're talking with people? Even when we're speaking directly from the heart we choose our words consciously and carefully, and while we're speaking we're aware of the effects our words are having on the people who hear them.

Helen Hayes – Laurence Olivier

Again, your double task as a performing artist is to be moved by the work of art you're performing—to immerse yourself completely in the work and to lose yourself, in a sense, and yet at all times to remain aware, objectively, of precisely what you're doing and how you're doing it. It's not easy, and sometimes the process, complicated to begin with, becomes downright mysterious. The year I graduated from the Juilliard School, our Commencement speaker was the celebrated actress Helen Hayes, and she told a story about Sir Laurence Olivier. Hayes was performing in a play with Olivier, and one night he gave a performance that was absolutely staggering. It was especially brilliant even for him. But after a slew of curtain calls Sir Laurence stormed off to his dressing room, slammed the door, and wouldn't let anybody in. When he finally allowed Miss Hayes into the room, she said, "What's the matter, Larry? You were magnificent tonight." And Olivier, still in a dark fury, pounded on a table and replied, "Yes I know. But that's just the problem. I don't know how I did it."

Sports-Music Connections

The efficient and graceful use of the body is crucial to both sports and musical performance. But there are many mental parallels as well, and the experiences of athletes can teach us quite a bit about what musicians do. Years ago I read an interview in The Washington Post with a professional baseball player named Charles Johnson. Johnson had hit a three-run homer to win a game, and this is what he said afterward: "I recognized a curveball right away, and told myself to stay on it. I wasn't trying to hit it out of the park, but I got a good part of the bat on it." Imagine, all that in the fraction of a second that the pitch was on its way. Imagine what that teaches us about the capacities of the human mind; what we learn about the startling speed of perception and thought, and about our ability to instantaneously connect thought to precise movements. And all of it directly applicable to issues in musical performance.

Interpretation – and the Metronome

Composers write pieces, and performers perform them. But for the performers, just about everything the composer writes, with the exception of the notes themselves, is a matter of interpretation. The composer indicates that a passage should be played softly? Fine. But *how* softly? It should get louder? Okay, but how *much* louder? Faster, slower? Same thing, it's a matter of interpretation and personal taste. And tastes and interpretations can change, sometimes from one performance to the next. Even when a composer indicates a specific tempo with a metronome marking—a certain number of clicks per minute—that's just a starting point, and composers themselves are famous for playing their own pieces at different tempos at different times, depending on how they happen to feel. "Feeling also has its tempo," wrote Beethoven. As for the metronome: "You know my views on the metronome," wrote Claude Debussy. "It might give the correct speed for one measure." And Johannes Brahms once wrote, "…the metronome is of no value… I have never believed that my blood and a mechanical instrument go well together."

The Music Lasts – Not the Interpretation

Anybody who's been around the music business for any length of time has met performers who are—how can I put this gently—legends in their own minds. Where the ego is large enough, the performer tends to think that the main reason a particular Beethoven sonata, or Tchaikovsky symphony, or Puccini opera is worth hearing is the brilliance of that performer's performance; no one else, after all, could possibly bring the work to life so wonderfully. Well, I'm all for musicians having appropriate levels of self-confidence, and indeed you should never take the stage unless you think you have something to offer, something personal. I've certainly always been aware that when I'm playing a concert, the quality of my performance is of great importance in bringing the music to life for the people who are in that particular audience. And if I play Mozart well, or Brahms, or Beethoven, I like to think I'm playing at least a small part in sustaining a vital and beautiful tradition. But there are performers who are so intent on proving *how* "personal" their interpretations are that they distort what great composers have written, and there are performers who conveniently forget that, before they started playing it, Beethoven's music, for example, had somehow managed to survive for quite some time already.

"Authentic Performance Practice" and The Colors of White

In 2004, the Vatican Museum presented an exhibit called *I colori del bianco*—"The Colors of White." What the exhibit showed, in a nutshell, is that our notion that the beauty of ancient Greek and Roman statues lies in their pure, white form is a relatively modern idea, with no basis in historical fact. Scientists working with electron microscopes discovered vestiges of all sorts of bright paint colors on ancient statues—colors that to modern eyes seem hideously garish—and the curators of the Vatican exhibit commissioned reproductions that were painted with those colors. The results were shocking, to say the least. Well, from there it's but a short step to the realization that our notions of "truth" in the history of *musical* ideas and so-called "authentic historical performance practice" may not always be quite as solid as we think, and also, perhaps, to the proposition that even if we *could* turn back the clock, we might not be comfortable with the results.

Bouncing Performers

You've probably seen classical music performers who bounce, or shake, or stomp, or fling their hair as far as it will go, or moan and groan in painful ecstasy while they play. And perhaps you've been intrigued, or dazzled, or distracted, or even, in some cases, revolted. And I imagine at some point you've asked yourself, "Am I watching something that's for real, something that is an artist's sincere and perhaps even unconscious physical expression of musical involvement, or is this all a lot of show biz baloney?" Well, I can tell you first of all that almost none of what you're seeing onstage is unconscious. A violinist who spends hours a day in the practice room adjusting finger movements by fractions of a millimeter is not unaware when she's tossing her hair, grimacing, or stomping her feet, any more than a professional pianist is somehow unaware that he's bouncing up and down on the bench. How much is too much, however, is up to you, the audience member. Does it help you enjoy the music, or does it get in the way? For me, as an audience member, the definition of "too much" is like the famous definition of pornography: I know it when I see it. When I find myself distracted from the music, when I feel that the performer's movements are aimed at showing off how wonderful, or beautiful, or sexy, or passionate the performer is—at showing off, in other words, pure and simple—rather than at expressing the essence of the music itself…that's when I feel a line has been crossed. I enjoy attractive and striking stage personalities and dynamic performances as much as the next person, but every bow stroke doesn't require a moan of ecstasy, and every piano bench shouldn't require a seatbelt. And after all, if the music is good enough and moving enough, the dynamism and the emotion don't have to be fake.

Heartless Performers

Many years ago I was having dinner with a group of colleagues when the name of a viola player we all knew came up. When I mentioned that this violist had just had his third heart attack, the instantaneous response from an old-timer across the table was, "Really? I didn't know he had a heart." As it happens, the heartless violist in question was not one of the finest players you're likely to meet. But we musicians have all known people we've found to be thoroughly unpleasant, even cruel, or thoroughly insipid and boring, who walk on stage and play or sing beautifully, movingly. This seems like a puzzle, or a paradox, but people are complex, and as much as we may sometimes hate to admit it, no one is a hundred percent awful. Warm hearts can beat under even the coldest exteriors. And luckily for all of us, where there's even a warm *corner* of a heart, it turns out it's usually susceptible to the beauties of music.

Music Teachers

It was George Bernard Shaw who famously wrote, "Those who can, do. Those who can't, teach." What Shaw forgot is that teaching is doing. And if you're looking for a group of people whose unlimited dedication is matched only by their extraordinary skills, I suggest you look no farther than public school music teachers. To me, these teachers are heroes. They take classrooms full of children from all walks of life and with hugely varying skill levels—sometimes starting as early as second grade—and day after day, with infinite patience, they teach the children how to play musical instruments, and then how to play them better and better. They give children the *gift* of music, and they teach the joy that comes from perseverance and accomplishment. Public school music teachers don't live for the thrill of seeing their names up in lights. They live for the light they see in their students' eyes, the kind of light that is lit by music.

What to Say After a (Bad) Concert

Has this ever happened to you? You go to a concert, and the concert is... awful. But the performer is someone you know, and you see that person afterward, and you have to say *something*. What can you say? Well, you can always start by looking the person straight in the eyes and saying, "What can I say?"

And there's always the classic, "I've never heard playing like that."

But here are some other possibilities, including a set of "Boy" choices:

"Boy, that Beethoven!"

"Boy, what a program!"

"Boy, you must be starving!"

"Boy, it's great to see you again!"

"You must really love Mozart!"

"Could you tell how much the audience loved it?"

"You should have been sitting where I was sitting."

"Thanks so much for the tickets!"

"What a crowd, eh?"

For sopranos, you can always depend on, "I *love* your gown," and for tenors, "Where will you be singing next?"

And my personal favorite, which must be accompanied by a hearty handshake and a direct, sincere look: "*Good* isn't the word."

So... feel free to use any of these, if you should ever need them, but please don't tell anyone you heard them from me.

What to Say After a (Bad) Concert, v. 2.0

In the unfortunate event that you've already used up your store of useful phrases, I thought I'd suggest a few more. The easiest thing to say is always a simple "Bravo." But of course it's a little *too* easy, and whenever someone has only said "bravo" to me after one of my concerts I've always been a bit suspicious.

A good thing to try is avoidance by misdirection, as in,

"Mozart! Don't you think it's the clarity that makes him so difficult?" Or, "I just *love* Schubert. And he died so *young*."

And when all else fails there's always "wow." Either alone, as in,

"Wow!" Or in combination, as in

"Wow, what a challenging program!" Or,

"Wow, you must be exhausted!" Or, perhaps best of all,

"Wow, you *did* it."

United Nations

One of the things I love most about the field of classical music is the way it brings together people from so many different countries. During the course of my career I've worked with musicians from the United States, the United Kingdom, Ireland, China, Taiwan, South Korea, Japan, the Philippines, Bulgaria, Hungary, Russia, Belarus, Poland, Israel, Sweden, Finland, Mexico, Venezuela, Colombia, Canada, France, Italy, Austria, and Germany. And I'm probably forgetting a few. Needless to say, the *governments* of all these countries haven't always gotten along so well. But in a lifetime of performing and teaching, I've never once witnessed an argument that had anything to do with where somebody was from, nor, for that matter, have I ever heard, among the musicians I've known, a single word of nationalist or racist invective. It's very simple and very beautiful: when musicians come together, they come together to make music.

Conceptions and Preconceptions in the Way

I attended a concert not long ago that featured a performance of a piece I've known and loved for decades. I'd been looking forward to the performance, but as it turned out, I didn't enjoy the performance, or the music, as much as I'd hoped I would, because I didn't like the interpretation. I simply couldn't free myself from my conception of how the music should go, not to mention how it shouldn't go. Afterward I shared my thoughts with another musician who, as it happened, was also somewhat disappointed, and we agreed that perhaps it's the non-musicians who are often the lucky ones, because they can listen with fresh ears, their experiences uncontaminated by preconceptions or technical judgments. Like it or not, performers can't help evaluating performance, especially in the cases of pieces we know or instruments we play. It's a strange phenomenon, but too often it's hard for musicians to just listen to the music.

Conflict

I won't mention any names, but many years ago there was a great string quartet that was famous for its members not getting along. People joked that it was a tragedy for this quartet if they showed up in a town that only had three hotels. I don't know if we can blame this particular quartet, but one theory that took hold was that the best results for chamber music groups are produced by conflict, and the resolution of conflict. I would like to on record as saying that I think this theory is a bunch of hooey. Maybe it worked for that one quartet, and maybe it even works for some others, but in my experience over many years, both playing and listening, I've always found that the best results come from agreement, from seeing and hearing things in similar ways. Musicians who fundamentally disagree can rehearse a piece twenty-five times and it won't make any difference. But like-minded musicians can rehearse for an hour and sound like they've been playing together for years.

Competitions

The careers of many famous musicians began with victories in international competitions. The composer Béla Bartók, however, once said, "Competitions are for horses, not artists," and he wasn't alone in thinking that Art is high and competition low, and that the reliability of competition results is dubious. At the risk of puncturing some preconceptions, though, I have to say that far more often than not, the musicians who win competitions are those who play the most beautifully. It's also true, however, that there are always people who play beautifully who *don't* win, which is very disturbing. Can it ever be right to call someone who plays music beautifully a "loser"? And isn't the price of competitions often the disillusion and discouragement of gifted musicians? Well, yes, it is. That's a real danger and a real drawback. The good news is that practice makes better, and win or lose, performers benefit enormously from the many hours of practice that come *before* the competitions. In musical competitions, as in competition in general, the costs and benefits are mixed.

Ear Training – Part 1

Ears can be trained. Which is why every music school in the world includes ear-training courses in its curriculum. I suppose it should go without saying, but for musicians the ability to recognize fine distinctions among sounds is crucial. And what musicians are trained to do is to recognize very specific kinds of information in sounds, to recognize relationships and patterns and to be able to reproduce them. They do this through practice and memorization. The distance in pitch between any two notes, for example, is called an interval. Well, musicians are trained to recognize intervals, no matter which two notes are involved, and to hear those intervals in advance, mentally, when they see those notes on a page, so that they can play or sing the notes correctly. With enough training, some very talented musicians can look at a complicated page of music and hear the whole thing, harmonies and all, in their heads, without playing a note.

Ear Training – Part 2

Every musician will tell you that there are some musicians who just seem to have better ears than others do. We're really talking about the connections in the brain, rather than about the actual organ of hearing, but in any case from the same sounds others hear, some people are able to extract more information, and they're able both to process and to store that information faster, more accurately, and more efficiently. Rigorous ear training courses can certainly lead to the development of great skills in hearing, great refinements. But individual differences do remain. Take perfect pitch, for example, also called absolute pitch. Play any note on the piano for a person with perfect pitch, and he can tell you what note it is. Ask a person with perfect pitch to sing a B-flat, or a C-sharp, and he can do it. Some have it, some don't. And training has never been able to fully explain it.

Musicians' Nightmares

I can't say for sure, but I would guess that most people have had what might be called recurring anxiety dreams, the kinds of dreams in which you find yourself in public with no clothes on, for example, or about to take a test in a subject you've never studied. People's anxiety dreams tend to be tailored to their particular personalities, circumstances, and experiences, and often to their particular professions. I've compared notes with a number of my musician colleagues, and based on my very un-scientific research, I can tell you that musicians' nightmares tend to fall into several familiar categories. There's the classic "being-onstage-with-no-clothes-on" dream, the "oh-no-my-alarm-didn't-go-off-and-it's-nine- o'clock-and the concert-started-at-eight" dream, the "I've-got-to-perform- this-piece-tonight-but-I've-never-looked-at-the-music-and-I-don't-know- how-it-goes" dream, and of course the "Yikes-I-left-my-instrument-in-the-restaurant" dream, which, a little too often, I'm afraid, turns out not to have been a dream.

Musicians' Injuries

There's very little that's natural about the physical positions and movements that are required to play most musical instruments. During the course of practicing and performing, a musician may repeat awkward movements literally thousands of times a day and millions of times a year, and maintain unnatural positions for untold numbers of hours. Muscle strain, tendinitis, nerve damage—all fall in the general category of "overuse" syndromes, and all are unfortunately extremely common among professional musicians. The good news is that improvements in position and technique, sometimes even small improvements, can make a big difference. I'm glad to say that these days more and more teachers, physical therapists, and doctors are focused on the problem of injuries and are helping musicians to find healthier ways to play their instruments.

Concert Etiquette

Concert etiquette is really just a matter of common sense and good manners. If you think you may be at risk of a coughing or sneezing fit, sit on the end of a row, not in the middle. If you're bringing a child to the concert and the child tends to fidget, sit in the back, not the front. Don't take pictures or make videos if you've been asked not to or if you may be blocking somebody else's view, and don't use a flash even if you *haven't* been asked not to. But etiquette is a two-way street, and performers need to have good manners too, and they should always respect the audience, who after all, are the only reason the performers are there to begin with. Sometimes people simply have to cough. So what? Performers should ignore it. Either that, or never perform during the winter. And if people clap between movements, that means they liked what they heard, which is a good thing. The appropriate response from the stage is an appreciative smile, not a snooty remark or a withering glance.

Conducting – Changes over the Centuries

The tools and techniques of conducting have changed a great deal over the centuries. In the Middle Ages and Renaissance, the people who led musical performances, especially vocal performances, usually simply waved their hands in the air to indicate the shape and speed of melodies—although sometimes they also held a long wooden staff in one hand and marked beats with it. During the Baroque period and into the early Classical period, larger instrumental ensembles were usually led by a harpsichord player waving a rolled-up piece of paper or parchment, or by the principal violinist of the group, waving his bow. It wasn't until the 19th century that orchestral conducting became a separate specialty, and that the *baton* became conductors' instrument of choice. And here's a strange fact: in early-19th-century opera performances, the conductor often stood right next to the stage facing the singers, but with his back to the orchestra.

Looking at Conductors?

A friend once asked me if orchestral musicians really look at the conductor when they're playing. It's an interesting question, because after all, how can you look at your music and play all the right notes if you're also looking up at the person waving the baton? The answer is that you do both, but not always in the same proportion and not always at the same time. There are times—the beginnings of pieces, for example, or at other times when the music starts or stops, or when the tempo changes—when you *have* to look directly at the conductor. And there are times when you have to concentrate entirely on playing the notes, especially in complicated or difficult sections—although one of the important skills you have to learn as an orchestral player is to somehow keep the conductor in view out of the corner of your eye at all times. Well, that's with good conductors. I hate to say it, but with bad conductors, it's usually better to look as little as possible.

Good Conductors

What makes a good conductor? Musical imagination and intelligence certainly come first, since there's no point in trying to communicate with an orchestra without ideas worth communicating. An excellent ear is essential, both for judging overall musical results and for pinpointing specific problems within large and complicated masses of sound, and so is a rock-solid sense of rhythm: tempos must be consistent, beating mistakes rare, and rhythmic complexities handled securely. A good conductor must also have a certain physical grace, or at least coordination, in order to produce a clear beat and musically meaningful gestures, and it almost goes without saying that a conductor will have enough personal presence and confidence to be a convincing, even inspiring leader. The ability to run an efficient rehearsal is crucial, too, and although this may seem obvious, with a good conductor both the music and the orchestra playing it will sound better after rehearsal than they did before. And like all good musicians, a conductor should have a flair for performance, the ability to bring something extra when it counts the most.

Bad Conductors

Now let's talk about bad conductors. Some bad conductors are unimaginative or uninteresting, and others are just not very gifted; they have difficulty communicating musical ideas, whether physically or verbally. Some may even put on quite an extravagant physical show, complete with rapturous facial expressions, but without showing much that's useful to the members of the orchestra. Other conductors are unprepared or undependable. They're uncertain in their gestures and cues, they make mistakes, and they use their time poorly in rehearsal. They may not even recognize problems, and when they do, they may not know how to fix them. To the extent they can, good orchestras try to ignore bad conductors, and it's not uncommon for orchestras to rescue bad conductors—to play passages correctly even when the conductor makes mistakes or gets lost. An excellent conductor is a great advantage for an orchestra, but it's a matter of professional accomplishment and pride for the best orchestras that they simply don't allow themselves to play below a certain level, no matter who's conducting.

Bad Old Days

In the bad old days of symphony orchestras in this country, orchestra musicians had few workplace protections. If a music director woke up in a bad mood, for example, and decided to fire an orchestra musician on the spot, he could, never mind that it might instantly deprive that musician of his livelihood. And some of the most famous conductors, unfortunately, were egotistical tyrants who inspired as much fear as admiration in the members of their orchestras. It wasn't until the 1960s, with a stronger national musicians' union and decent collective bargaining agreements, that professional orchestra players could begin to count on reasonable job security and salaries and working conditions appropriate to their extraordinary skills. And it's worth emphasizing that the musical results with orchestras that are treated fairly and decently by their managements and music directors are every bit as good, if not better, than they were in the bad old days.

Toscanini – Anger Management

I came across a collection of the letters of Arturo Toscanini, and in the Introduction, the editor mentions that one could write "a whole psychology textbook" on the subject of Toscanini and anger. Well all I can say is that if there *had* been such a textbook, it would have been a good idea for Toscanini to have read it. He may have been a great conductor, but he was also an ill-tempered tyrant. In his day, conductors had absolute power over their orchestras, so Toscanini never had to control his temper the way most people have to in civilized society. He could indulge his temper, and he did, often screaming at orchestras and treating orchestra musicians with great cruelty. Was he the only conductor to act this way? Certainly not. There's a long list. Is such behavior indeed a symptom of psychological problems, of unresolved neuroses? Yes, it is. And let's be clear: cruelty to musicians may once have been tolerated, but it's not necessary for great music-making, and it never has been.

Touring with Orchestras

When professional orchestras went on tour in the old days, 50 years ago or more, management stayed in the nice hotels, and orchestra members were put up in the second-rate hotels. Things have certainly changed. These days, if you're a player in a top orchestra, you stay in top hotels, no matter what country you're traveling in, and you almost never have to carry your own suitcase. You don't even have to carry your own instrument, because the instruments get transported in fancy packing cases. Some things haven't changed, though. Touring is still tiring. It's true that musicians are lucky to get to travel, and to get to know places they might otherwise never have visited. It's one of the great benefits of being a musician. But playing concerts in different cities every night, changing time zones, changing languages, changing climates, figuring out what to eat, getting on and off buses and trains and planes… it's not quite as glamorous as it may seem. And especially for the stage crews, the people who have to load and unload the planes and trucks and set up and break down in every city, touring is *much* harder than just playing concerts at home.

Pablo de Sarasate

On January 2, 1881, the Spanish violinist Pablo de Sarasate was in Paris to play the premiere of the Violin Concerto No. 3 by Camille Saint-Saëns. Now perhaps that doesn't strike you as the most important event in music history. But suppose I also told you that in 1875 Sarasate had been in Paris to play the premiere of the *Symphonie Espagnole* by Édouard Lalo; that in 1878 he'd played the premiere of Max Bruch's Violin Concerto No. 2; and that not only were the Saint-Saëns, the Lalo, and the Bruch all written for him, but so too were the Bruch *Scottish Fantasy*, the Saint-Saëns *Introduction and Rondo Capriccioso*, and the Wieniawski Violin Concerto No. 2. Pablo de Sarasate, in other words, was a critical figure in the history of the 19th-century violin concerto, a brilliant virtuoso whose breathtaking abilities inspired the composition of great and lasting works.

Paul Wittgenstein – and Ravel

Great works of art have been born under strange and even tragic circumstances. During World War I, the Austrian concert pianist Paul Wittgenstein (the older brother of the philosopher Ludwig Wittgenstein) was shot in the elbow, and his right arm was amputated. If the bullet had missed, the history of music would have been different. After the war, Wittgenstein was determined to continue his concert career, and he commissioned a number of famous composers to write works in which the pianist played with the left hand alone. Among those composers were such famous names as Sergei Prokofiev, Paul Hindemith, Franz Schmidt, Benjamin Britten, and Erich Wolfgang Korngold, all of whom fulfilled their commissions and enriched what had been a very limited repertoire. But the most remarkable contribution to this repertoire was made by another famous composer Wittgenstein commissioned, Maurice Ravel. Ravel's Concerto in D Major for the Piano, Left Hand, is not just a fine piece for the left hand, it's one of the masterpieces of the piano literature. Paul Wittgenstein and the Vienna Symphony Orchestra played the premiere of this great work on January 5, 1932.

IPA

Professional singers often have to sing in languages with which they're completely unfamiliar. And yet they're expected to pronounce all the words correctly. How do they do it? Well, they certainly can, and do, work with coaches who are native speakers, but most often they start by studying the foreign words with something called the International Phonetic Alphabet, or IPA, for short. The IPA was invented in the late 1880s by a group of English and French language teachers, or "phoneticians," and it consists of the standard letters of the Latin alphabet, modified versions of those letters, symbols and accents that are called diacritics, or diacritical markings, which are used in conjunction with the letters, and other signs and markings. The IPA is remarkably versatile, but if it sounds complicated, it is, and singers often have to learn a whole new set of symbols when they're learning a piece in a new language.

Lefty Violinists

Have you ever seen a lefty violinist? I've heard of a few, but in my whole life I've only met one string player who holds the bow in the left hand and the instrument in the right. I don't really know how the tradition of playing "righty" got started, but it hasn't changed for hundreds of years. Why can't lefties just reverse the strings and play the way they like? Well, it's not that simple. A violin (or viola, cello, or double bass) may look perfectly symmetrical from the outside, but on the inside it's not symmetrical at all. There's a strip of wood called the bass bar, for example, that's glued inside the top of the instrument to the *left* of center, and a wooden dowel, called the soundpost, wedged between the top and back to the *right* of center. Perhaps more importantly, the top and back of the instrument are carved to different thicknesses at different points, and the fine shadings of thickness are not precisely symmetrical from left to right. It's hard to overcome tradition, and even harder to overcome asymmetry.

Second Violin

The second violin part in a composition such as a string quartet or symphony is an individual musical line that forms part of the fabric of the piece. In a string quartet, one person plays the second violin part, while in an orchestra, all the members of the second violin section play the second violin part. A person playing a second violin part might say, "I'm playing second violin," or simply, "I'm playing second," and in this sense "second violin" describes a position in a group, just as "second base" describes a position on a baseball team. The second violin part tends to be less prominent than the first violin part; often, for example, it provides an accompaniment while the first violin part carries the melody. But though the term "playing second fiddle" has become a synonym for playing a subordinate role, a violin is a violin, and you've got to make it sound good no matter which part you're playing. Second violin parts are often extremely demanding, and when it comes to professional ensembles it's a mistake to assume that someone playing second violin is a less accomplished musician than someone playing first.

Bad Chairs

Imagine you're a professional basketball player about to take a foul shot. You've practiced this thousands of times, and you know exactly how you need to set your feet and orient your body in order to get the best results. But then you notice that the floor is uneven, or slippery, or has a big depression right at the foul line, or has a board sticking up under your foot. It's going to be much harder to make the shot. Well, this doesn't actually happen on professional basketball courts. But something like it does happen to professional musicians on tour—all too often, in fact—and it's called "bad chairs." Chairs that are too low, too high, too hard, too slippery, or with seats tilted backward: they're the bane of musicians' existence. After playing a whole concert on a bad chair you often wind up with a dreadful backache, but more importantly, when you can't sit right, it's much harder to play your best.

Funny Things that Happen on Stage

Musicians tell lots of stories about funny things that have happened on stage during concerts. Often the stories are about disasters or near-disasters, and to be honest, they usually seem much funnier later on than the events themselves felt when they were actually happening. But one of the funniest stories I know isn't about a disaster. It was told to me by the former second violinist of a well-known string quartet. The quartet had played a concert one night, had been up very late, and had driven for hours to play a concert the next night, with no time to rest. One of the pieces on the program was a contemporary work in one section of which the second violin part consisted of one note played softly and held endlessly. Well, you guessed it. While the violinist held the note, bow on the string, he fell sound asleep. And of course the funniest thing is that, because of the style of the music, nobody noticed.

Forgotten Performers

In 1918, the music critic Olin Downes published a book called *The Lure of Music*. It's a collection of biographical sketches of famous composers, and it includes listening suggestions, samples of the composers' works on Columbia records. Most of the composers Downes writes about, people such as Verdi, Chopin, Berlioz, and Dvořák, are among the immortals. They were famous then and they'll always remain famous. But what's striking to me is that, among the *performers* on the recording, I know hardly any of the names. Oscar Seagle, Kathleen Parlow, Orville Harrold, Hulda Laschanska, Florencio Constantino? I had never heard of them, but they must have been a big deal in their time for Columbia to have recorded them. The lesson here, and it's a good one for today's performers to remember, if only to keep their egos from swelling too grandly, is that performers and performances come and go, but what lasts is the music.

Outdoor Concerts – The Puppy

Outdoor concerts can be delightful, especially when the music and the natural surroundings make a perfect mix. Then again, when you're playing outdoors, things sometimes happen that wouldn't ever happen in the concert hall. And I'm not just talking about thunderstorms. I'm thinking of a concert I played many years ago at a festival in France. The setting was beautiful—we were in a valley in the Alps—and the music was Franz Schubert's "Trout" Quintet. What could be better? The performance received an unexpected interruption, however, when a Labrador retriever puppy decided to run up on stage and say hello to all the musicians, wiggling his cute little hind quarters at the audience the whole time. It wasn't, perhaps, what Schubert had in mind, but everybody laughed, and it certainly made the concert unforgettable. Well, not everybody laughed, actually. The puppy made his entrance in the middle of a cello solo. Our cellist was a terribly serious chap, as I recall, and he was *not* amused.

Traveling – Touring

Do you find traveling glamorous? Sitting around in airports, waiting in lines, carrying luggage, eating in unfamiliar places, sleeping in unfamiliar beds? Well imagine doing that for about ten months a year, and imagine doing it alone, while having to prove, over and over again every single week, that you're one of the best in the world at what you do. And when you've imagined all that, and added in lots more hours spent alone practicing, you've imagined the glamorous life of a touring soloist. Talk with today's artists and then read the letters of famous musicians from long ago and you'll notice a common thread: fatigue. The saving grace? The music. Big paychecks are nice, of course, but thank goodness for the music. Because when a performer is on stage, fatigue is forgotten, and there's no more "place"—no Hong Kong or Helsinki or Houston. The music becomes the musician's whole world.

Calluses

I'm guessing you haven't thought much about this, but one of the things we musicians have to put up with is calluses. Not feeling sympathetic? But what if the calluses are peeling, or bleeding, or have bruises under or around them, or make you look like you've been attacked by a vampire? You can probably guess that string players have calluses on the tips of the fingers of their left hands, and you've seen the indelible marks on the necks of violinists and violists. But did you know that cellists sometimes have calluses on their chests from where their instruments lean against them, and that clarinetists and oboists can get painful calluses on their right thumbs from where they support the weight of their instruments, and that brass players can get calluses on their lips? And the poor harpists! If a harpist happens to take a vacation, and she lets her calluses get soft, getting back into shape can be exquisitely painful. Harpists may sound like angels, but bleeding fingertips are not very angelic.

Virtuoso

Virtuosos have played an extremely important role in the history of music. They've expanded our horizons, our ideas of the possible, and in doing so they've influenced or inspired the work of countless composers. The word "virtuoso" is from the Latin *virtus*, meaning "worth," or "excellence." It can be a noun, as in "violin virtuoso," or an adjective, as in "virtuoso violinist." A basic requirement for a virtuoso is an extraordinary technical facility, the ability to play extremely difficult music, especially fast music, with apparent ease. And indeed, one of the main reasons virtuosos have always fascinated audiences is that the speed of their physical movements is far beyond the scale of everyday human experience. None of our everyday movements can match the speed of a virtuoso's fingers. Music involves more than physical challenges and stopwatches, though, and the true virtuoso is someone who combines flash and dash with musical substance and understanding: someone, in other words, who demonstrates not just the ability to play fast, but the ability to play beautifully.

Franz Liszt – Part 1

In 1841, Franz Liszt played three concerts in Paris, and afterward he wrote, "My… solo recitals…are unrivalled concerts, such as I *alone* can give in Europe at the present moment… Without vanity or self-deception, I think I may say that an effect so striking, so complete, so irresistible had never before been produced by an instrumentalist in Paris." Well, if it's true it ain't braggin', as they say, and by all accounts it *was* true. The poet Heinrich Heine called the effect "Lisztomania." Others called it "Liszt fever," "a *contagion*," one critic wrote, "that breaks out in every city our artist visits." Before Liszt, when pianists played solo works, it was always as part of mixed programs, programs that included other music and other musicians. Liszt himself invented the solo piano recital, and he coined the term "recital," too.

Franz Liszt – Part 2

The frenzied reactions of Franz Liszt's audiences may have been known as "Lisztomania," or "Liszt fever," but Liszt's recitals were not just virtuoso flash with little substance. Liszt had a huge repertoire; he certainly played his own showpieces, but he also played pieces by all the great composers of the day and by those he called the "classics," including many works of Bach, Mozart, and Beethoven. And by all accounts he played these pieces wonderfully. Felix Mendelssohn, for example, once said, "I have never seen a musician whose feeling for music filled him to the very finger-tips and flowed directly out from them, as it does with Liszt." And even Johannes Brahms, whose own style of piano playing was apparently the polar opposite of Liszt's, was once heard to say, "Whoever has not heard Liszt cannot even speak of piano playing."

Needless Comparisons

I remember hearing two remarkably gifted young musicians play a concert some time ago. One was a nineteen-year-old pianist and one a sixteen-year-old violinist. And it was pretty humbling, because when I was nineteen, I wasn't nearly as accomplished as either the nineteen-year-old or the sixteen-year-old. But I didn't quit when I was nineteen, or even when I was in my early twenties and only too well aware that I was still far from a finished product—and eventually I was able to make a career as a professional musician. The lesson here, a hard one to learn, but one that I've always tried to teach my students, is that everyone makes progress at his or her own pace, and what's crucial is *where* you eventually arrive, not how fast you get there. Early accomplishment is wonderful, and sometimes even amazing. But comparing yourself to others can be needlessly discouraging. If people are enjoying your performance now, they won't care whether you blossomed at thirteen or at thirty.

Practicing

When I was a little boy just starting violin lessons, my teacher's instructions were that I should practice a half hour every day. For a six-year-old, or this particular one, anyway, this seemed a large load. I liked the violin, but a whole half hour, every day? Usually I would start, and then run to my mother every five minutes asking, "Is it a half hour yet?" And even later, when I started on the road to a career in music, practicing remained a duty, something I knew I had to do even if I would rather have been doing something else. And now? Well, amid all of life's accumulated burdens and time-consuming obligations, practicing has come to seem a luxury and a delight. It's quite a change. I still have to practice, but now I love to practice. All I have to do is find a few free hours and presto, the world turns into music! I play my viola, and I try to get better.

Master Classes

A master class is a public lesson. A distinguished teacher—that would be the master—works with a student on a piece of music, but the teacher isn't the student's regular teacher, and instead of the lesson taking place in a private studio, it takes place in front of an audience. It's a kind of double performance: the student is performing for the audience, but so is the teacher. And the idea is that whatever the teacher has to offer will be of value both to the student and to the observers. My own feeling is that the best master classes are the ones where the student is exposed to ideas and principles that go beyond a single piece of music. The class should help the student be a better musician, a more comfortable and convincing interpreter no matter what the piece. And the best teachers are supportive. I've seen famous musicians stoke their own egos by humiliating students in master classes, and even bringing them to tears. But *good* teachers never do that.

Principles of Teaching

In the world of instrumental and vocal teaching, most teachers approach their work with certain basic principles in mind. For me, one of those principles is that whether we're dealing with individuals or with ensembles, there's no separating "technical" goals from musical goals. I don't believe, in other words, that it makes sense just to learn the notes first and then somehow to "plug in" the music later. Sure, there are certain fundamental techniques that all beginners have to master, but after that it's only by having musical goals—goals of expressivity, vitality, and beauty—that we discover what we need to be able to do technically to reach those goals. And technical accomplishment by itself, after all, is of little interest: I usually get a laugh from my students when I stress that no audience member has ever left a concert quivering with excitement because a performance was "correct."

Changing Habits – Mark Twain

One of the things I've learned as a string teacher is that good habits can often replace a student's bad habits quickly, because the good habits make playing easier. But it was Mark Twain, strangely enough, who helped me to realize that the switch can only result from a very conscious and rational process on the student's part, a process of understanding and acceptance. In his essay "Taming the Bicycle," Twain wrote, "In order to keep my position, a good many things were required of me, and in every instance the thing required was against nature. Against nature, but not against the laws of nature. That is to say, that whatever the needed thing might be, *my* nature [and] habit…moved me in one way, while some immutable and unsuspected law of physics required that it be done in just the other way… The intellect has to come to the front, now. It has to teach the limbs to discard their old education and adopt the new."

Jascha Heifetz's American Debut

On October 27, 1917, the great violinist Jascha Heifetz made his American debut in Carnegie Hall. I say "great"—many people would call Heifetz the greatest, a violinist who dazzled audiences with his stupendous technical ability, melted hearts with his gorgeous tone, and inspired thousands of young musicians to play more beautifully than they ever thought they could. Heifetz was only sixteen years old when he made his American debut, but he had been a world-famous virtuoso since at least the age of eleven, which is when he made his debut as soloist with the Berlin Philharmonic Orchestra. The reviews of the Carnegie Hall concert were sensational, and two weeks after the concert Heifetz made his first recordings for the Victor Talking Machine Company. Those recordings, which are wonderful, are still available, as are the hundreds of other recordings that Heifetz later made for RCA Victor.

Pablo Casals

Pablo Casals, called *Pau* Casals in his native Catalan language, was born on December 29, 1876, and he lived for almost a century, dying in 1973. Casals began his professional career in 1895 playing cello in a theater orchestra in Paris, but he didn't stay there long, and by the time he was twenty-five, he was well on his way to recognition as the greatest cellist of his era. Many consider him among the greatest cellists of *any* era, and he was also a conductor and composer. Casals was a man of immense personal magnetism, and through his playing, his teaching, his conducting, and his recordings—especially his recordings of the solo cello suites of J. S. Bach—he inspired generation after generation of musicians. He once said, "They call me a great cellist. I am not a cellist. I am a musician. That is much more important."

Mstislav Rostropovich

I had the enormous good fortune as a young man to get to work with Mstislav Rostropovich (1927-2007). Rostropovich was the foremost cello virtuoso of his time, and the dedicatee for many of the most important cello works of the second half of the 20th century, works by such composers as Dmitri Shostakovich, Sergei Prokofiev, Benjamin Britten, Henri Dutilleux, and Krzysztof Penderecki. Rostropovich, or "Slava," as everybody called him, was the music director of the National Symphony Orchestra when I played in that ensemble, and with all his other engagements, he still somehow made time to give master classes just for members of the orchestra. I learned a tremendous amount from him, and to this day I don't seem to be able to give a master class myself without quoting Slava at least several times—especially since he could be extremely funny. One time, for example, he was stressing the importance of finding variety in sound color, but rather than wax poetic he simply said (with a strong Russian accent that's impossible to reproduce in writing), "Even if it's beautiful, if the sound stays the *same,* pretty soon the guy in the audience says to the guy next to him, 'Where are *you* going for dinner?' and the other guy says, 'Oh. I don't know. Where are you going for dinner?'" Mstislav Rostropovich: a monumental artist and a marvelous teacher.

Robert Mann

Performers are always seeking the most effective and compelling ways to bring a composer's musical ideas to life. I stress the plural, "ways," because there's never just one way. Some musicians sometimes forget this, unfortunately, but the best musicians, and the best *teachers* never do. When I was a graduate student, the string quartet I played in was working on a Bartók string quartet, and our faculty coach was Robert Mann, founder and first violinist of the Juilliard Quartet. Now, if ever there was a musician who was entitled to say of a Bartók quartet, "This is the way it goes," it was Robert Mann. He knew those quartets inside out, and had recorded them more than once. But he never imposed his ideas. He was much more interested in *our* ideas, and how we might best articulate and convey them—and that's one of the reasons he was not just a superb performer, but also a great teacher.

Old 78s

Have you by any chance been hanging on to your grandparents' old 78-rpm records? Carting them around, perhaps, and storing them on shelves or in boxes whenever you've moved from place to place? And perhaps thinking or hoping that after a hundred years your carefully preserved recordings of such fabulously famous artists as Enrico Caruso, Nellie Melba, and Mischa Elman must surely be valuable? Well, I've got good news and bad news for you. The good news is that you're fortunate to have lovely relics of an age gone by, and reminders of the efforts of great artists. The bad news is that, if you're talking dollars and cents, the records most likely have almost no value. And the reason is simple: there are lots of them. And that's putting it mildly. Caruso alone made around 260 recordings and sold millions of copies. It *is* possible to find a rare 78, but it's, well, rare.

Tenors

The word "tenor" is from the Latin *tenere*, "to hold," and in medieval and Renaissance vocal music, from about 1250 to 1500, the tenor voice was the "holding voice." It was the voice that held the principal melody, often with long held-out notes, and the voice around which the other voices were composed. The tenor voice, always a male voice, was not necessarily a high voice, or at least not originally. And the meaning of "tenor" actually varied from place to place. But it seems that by the 1400s and 1500s, the term "tenor" did generally mean a high male voice, and it was the voice that was usually featured in popular songs and early opera. By the mid-1600s, though, the castrati—singing eunuchs—had become the unchallenged stars of opera, and it wasn't until the late 1700s and early 1800s that the brilliant operatic tenor as we know him today came into his own.

Page Turners – Part 1

Have you ever wondered why pianists need page turners? They're not, after all, the only ones who use both hands to play their instruments. The answer is that piano music goes by too fast: you can only fit about half as much music on one page of piano music as you can on one page of music for a non-keyboard instrument. And that's for the simple reason that in printed piano music, each line of music takes up *two* lines, one for the left hand one for the right. Each set of two lines together, for left hand and right, is called a "system." And I should mention that in piano scores for chamber music, you can fit far *less* than half as much music per page, because the parts for the other instrument or instruments are also included, printed above each system in smaller notes just above the notes for the piano. To give you an example: in one edition of the Brahms Piano Quartet No. 2 that I'm familiar with, the violin part is 17 pages-long, while the piano score covers 64 pages.

Page Turners – Part 2

Turning pages for pianists is a pretty thankless job. The page turner is usually only noticed when he or she messes up. But for pianists who depend on page turners— and at some point most pianists do, at least those who haven't switched over to electronic tablets—good, dependable, unobtrusive page turners are worth their weight in gold. They free the pianists from worry and make their lives much easier. Then again, virtually every pianist has a collection of page turner stories that are either funny or horrible or both. Examples? Well, I'm not a pianist, but I was onstage once with a page turner who had eaten a pre-concert dinner very heavy with onion and garlic, and it was all our pianist could do to keep from passing out from the man's breath. We also once had a page turner, who while leaning over and trying to turn a page during the concert, said to our pianist, "I had an operation on my shoulder. It wasn't successful."

Bel Canto – Gioacchino Rossini

I wonder what today's voice teachers would think of the composer Gioacchino Rossini's ideas for a vocal training curriculum. According to Rossini, learning the art of bel canto, or "beautiful singing," should begin with many months of *soundless* exercises, starting no later than the age of twelve. Next, several years of just scales, in order to achieve consistency of sound quality over the whole range of the voice. Then three years of vocalises and exercises to learn specific techniques for agility and fluidity, and finally, after having assimilated the results of all that work, three years of real singing. But even then training isn't finished, because the singer has to have an education in "Style," which for Rossini meant studying the traditions embodied in the performances of the great singers who had come before, and who were justly famous. Rossini himself was a child prodigy, and was composing excellent pieces by the age of twelve. Wonderfully talented but also famously (or supposedly) lazy, he retired at the age of thirty-seven. Still, over the course of his relatively brief career, he composed 39 operas and became arguably the most famous composer in the world. When he was thirty, in 1822, he met Beethoven, who wrote him a note that said, "Ah, Rossini. So you're the composer of *The Barber of Seville*. I congratulate you. It will be played as long as Italian opera exists."

Rossini on Singers

In *Il barbiere di Siviglia* ("The Barber of Seville") and his many other operas, Gioacchino Rossini (1792-1868) gave singers plenty of opportunities to show off their talents. But in a letter he wrote in 1851, Rossini made it clear that he didn't have much patience for the *cult* of the great singer, or for singers whose pretensions got the better of them. "To fulfil his part properly," Rossini wrote, "the good singer needs only to be a capable interpreter of the ideas of…the composer, trying to express them to full effect and bring them out in the clearest light… In short, the composer and the poet are the only serious *creators*. Some skilful singers occasionally try to show off with additional embellishments; and if this is to be called creative, well and good; but it is a form of creative work which is quite often unsuccessful and frequently spoils the composer's ideas, robbing them of the simplicity of expression they were intended to have."

Prima Donna

Of the many musical terms that have made their way into general usage, one of the most colorful, and useful, is *prima donna*. These days the term gets applied to anyone with an oversized ego, man or woman, but in Italian it simply means "first lady," and it's been in use since the 1600s as the title for the singer of an opera's principal female role. By the 1700s the term was already associated with the artistic and commercial cult of the glamorous leading lady—a cult that met with little protest from the leading ladies themselves—and some prima donnas demanded to be called *prima donna assoluta* ("absolute leading lady"). In the bad old days, some prima donnas even hired claques to cheer them and throw flowers, and to boo and hiss other singers. The world of opera still produces the occasional impossible prima donna, it's true, but let's face it, you can find prima donnas in any field.

Joanna Maurer – Age Differences

Joanna Maurer plays violin in the Metropolitan Opera Orchestra, and for almost twenty years she's been my colleague in the American Chamber Players. She's a remarkable musician, and for all these years I've been inspired both by her beautiful violin playing and by what I might call her musical wisdom—her interpretive insights and her mastery of the craft of chamber music. And like all her colleagues, I've benefited from her personal wisdom, as well: Joanna doesn't just help people solve problems, she helps people avoid them. But here's what's funny. This friend and colleague, this person whose musicianship and wisdom I've relied on for so long, is almost a quarter century younger than I am. And I think this is an example of one of the wonderful aspects of life as a musician: age differences don't mean anything. What counts is what kind of person you are, and how you make music.

U.S. Marine Band

Some years ago I had the privilege of appearing as viola soloist with the United States Marine Band, "the Presidents Own," and I can tell you that it was a great experience. Like the members of the other premier service bands, the bands of the Army, Navy, Air Force, and Coast Guard, the Marine Band players are graduates of some of the nation's top conservatories, and they're terrific musicians. And they include great string players, too, not just winds, brass, and percussion. I think the string players are probably happiest on the occasions the Marine Band plays classical repertoire, but go to YouTube and check out the performance of "The Stars and Stripes Forever" by two violinists from the USMB, and I promise you'll be knocked out. The musicians of "The President's Own" are trained to carry themselves like Marines, but the one big advantage they have over the musicians of the other service bands, and of other Marine Corps bands, is that they don't have to go through boot camp.

IV. INSTRUMENTS

Flutist - Flautist

In America, 99.9 percent of the people who play the flute for a living call themselves flutists, not flautists. That's not a scientific number, but I think it's pretty
accurate. In any case, I've never heard any American flute playing colleague refer to
herself as anything *but* a flutist, so please don't ever worry about sounding uncul-
tured or unsophisticated if that's the term you use. And where does the word "flautist" come from, anyway? After all, the instrument is called the flute, not the flaut.
Well, it comes from the Italian word for flute, which is *flauto*. "Flautist" is certainly
a correct term, but it's far more commonly heard in the British Isles, where it's
pronounced "flawtist," than it is here. And if by some chance you'd like to wax
historical, the term you'll want to use is "fluter." Fluter is now archaic, but it was
around long before either flutist *or* flautist.

Piano

I always enjoy telling the story of how the piano got its name. *Piano* means "soft," in Italian, and it seems a little strange that an instrument that can weigh almost a thousand pounds and compete in volume with a symphony orchestra should be called a "soft." Well, we have to start with the piano's predecessor, the harpsichord, or *gravicembalo*, in Italian. When you press the keys on a harpsichord, you cause the instrument's strings to be plucked, not struck, and no matter how hard, or how softly, you press the keys, the sound volume stays the same. You can't, in other words, get gradually louder or softer as you play—you can't make *crescendos* or *diminuendos*. And especially if you're playing on a harpsichord with a single keyboard (some harpsichords have two keyboards, or two "manuals"), you can't play a melody in the right hand louder than an accompaniment in the left. But in about 1700, an Italian named Bartolomeo Cristofori invented a keyboard instrument with little hammers that strike the strings, and now by varying your touch on the keys you *could* vary the volume. Cristofori called his instrument the *gravicembalo col' piano e forte*—the "harpsichord with soft and loud." Eventually this lengthy name got shortened to *pianoforte*, and from there it was just a short step to "piano" all by itself. Devotees of "authentic performance practice" may not like to hear this, but for most musicians of the late 1700s, the supplanting of the harpsichord by the piano represented progress, a triumph over the harpsichord's limitations. Keyboard music of the Classical Era and beyond, beginning with the piano sonatas of Haydn, Mozart, and Beethoven, would not even have been conceivable on the harpsichord.

Violin – Fiddle – Vidula – Fidula

What's the difference between a violin and a fiddle? Well, I've heard it said that a violin has strings and a fiddle has "strangs." But in reality, violin and fiddle are just two different words for the same instrument, and classical violinists use the term fiddle all the time. A classical violinist might call a priceless Stradivarius, for example, "a terrific fiddle." And it may surprise you that the word *fiddle* was in common use long before the word *violin*. Neither the modern word violin nor the instrument to which it refers was in standard use until the 1500s, but musicians played on a variety of instruments known as fiddles during the Middle Ages and the Renaissance. *Violino*, which is Italian for "violin," is the diminutive form of *viola*, which from the 1400s until the 1700s was the Italian generic term for any bowed string instrument. The word *viola* itself came from the Old French *viole*, which came from the Provençal *viula*, which came from the Medieval Latin *vidula*. I used to think, as others did, that the word *fiddle* also came from *vidula*. Pronounce the V in vidula in the German style, as an F, and, voilà! *Vidula* becomes *fidula*, which is awfully close to fiddle. I've since discovered, however, that things are probably the other way around. It turns out that the word *Fidula* is first found in Old High German in the 9th century, 200 years before the word *vidula* appears in Medieval Latin. So where did *vidula* come from? That seems to be a bit of a mystery.

How the Cello Got its Name

Up until the 1700s, the Italian term for any stringed instrument played with a bow was viola. *Viola da braccio*, or "arm viola," was the generic name for any member of what came to be the modern violin family. The instrument we now call the cello was first called the *basso di viola da braccio*, or "bass arm viola," because, even though it was always played between the legs, it was a member of the modern violin family, not the *viola da gamba* ("leg" viola) family. So where did the word *cello* come from? Believe it or not, it comes from an Italian word meaning "little big viola." In Italian, the suffix *–one* (pronounced "oh-nay") means big, and the suffix *–ello*, or *–cello* (pronounced "chello") means small (as in Monticello – "little mountain"). If you add *–one* to *viola*, you get *violone*, "big viola," which was an early name for the double bass. But the "bass arm viola" was smaller than the *violone*, so a diminutive had to be added, turning *violone*, the "big viola," into *violoncello*, the "*little* big viola." And in English, it was but a short hop from violoncello to 'cello, and then to plain cello. I should add that although the word violoncello is still seen quite frequently in British programs, American cellists almost universally refer to their instrument as the cello.

Violin and Viola Sizes – and Concert Attire

The body length of a full-size violin is about 14 inches, give or take a very small fraction. This is a standard length, and an optimum length, arrived at by trial and error over many years by the great violin makers of history. Violas, on the other hand, have no standard length. For the pitch range and acoustics of the viola there probably is an optimum length, but whatever it is, it's way too great for the instrument still to be held up and played under the chin. Body lengths of violas vary anywhere from under 15 inches, for very small instruments, to over 18 inches, for huge ones. My own viola has a body length of about 16¾ inches, and frankly I wish it were smaller, because it would be easier to play. A major problem for me in concert performances, for years, was the awful sensation that my viola was about to slip out from under my chin and off my shoulder. I found accessories that helped—a good chinrest and a good shoulder rest for support—but the best step I ever took was simply to stop playing in suit jacket, tuxedo, or tailcoat. The idea was to remove all encumbrances. Even a turtleneck is more fabric than I like to have between me and the viola, because every layer of fabric pushes the instrument a little farther away, makes me stretch my arm a little more, and makes the instrument feel less secure. What's funny is that when it comes to concert dress I'm still something of a traditionalist, and I wear all black. But now I'm a traditionalist without a collar. And why don't I just buy a smaller instrument? Well, unless you get very lucky, it's hard to find a small viola that can produce a big sound.

Violin Family – Into the Woods

The members of the modern violin family—the violin, viola, cello, and double bass—are made of wood. But on any one instrument you may find four or even five different *kinds* of wood. The top, also called the "table," or "belly" of the instrument, will be made of spruce—a strong, light, but soft wood. The back, and the sides—which are also called the ribs—will almost always be made of maple, which is a very hard wood. Maple is also the wood from which the scroll, the neck, and the bridge are carved. The wood that runs under the strings, called the fingerboard, is generally made of ebony, which is an extremely hard wood, and the tuning pegs, which hold the strings at one end, and the tailpiece, which holds them at the other, may be carved from ebony, rosewood, or boxwood. For violins and violas, ebony, rosewood, and boxwood are the woods of choice for the chinrest, too.

Stradivarius

Several centuries ago, it was common for violin makers to print their names in Latin on the paper labels they glued in their instruments. That's what the great Italian violin maker Antonio Stradivari did, and that's why an instrument made by Stradivari is known as a *Stradivarius*. Stradivari was born around 1644, and he died ninety-three years later, in 1737. He learned his craft as an apprentice to Nicolò Amati, and it was Amati's grandfather, Andrea Amati, working back in the 1500s, who's thought to have perfected the form of the modern violin. Stradivari is certainly known best for his violins—he probably made at least a thousand of them, and about six hundred fifty have survived—but there are still somewhere around 55 Stradivarius cellos in existence, and 11 or 12 violas. Stradivari also made mandolins and guitars—two of his guitars have survived—and probably harps and lutes, as well.

Old Tools, Old Instruments

I don't suppose you have a pair of 400-year-old pliers in your kitchen tool drawer, or a screwdriver made in the 1700s? No, probably not. Tools don't tend to last that long. The tools of string players, though, are an entirely different story. I've played many concerts with a violinist whose violin was made in about 1600 and whose bow probably dates from the late 1700s, and with a cellist whose 345-year-old cello is one of the most remarkable instruments I've ever heard. My own viola isn't terribly old—it was made in the mid-twentieth century—but my bow was made in about 1860 and has been in continuous use ever since. Sometimes in rehearsals I can't help smiling just from looking around at my colleagues' instruments and bows and thinking about how far these old tools have traveled, in whose hands, and how much great music they've played.

Pizzicato

There are many musical terms that get translated into several languages, depending on the native language of the composer who's using the terms. The Italian term *allegro*, for example, might appear as "lively," in English, or *vif,* in French, or *lebhaft,* in German. But there's one musical term that for some reason you'll only ever see, or hear, in the original Italian, and that's *pizzicato* (pronounced "pitz-ee-cahtoe"). Pizzicato is the Italian word for "plucked." To play pizzicato on a stringed instrument means to make the notes sound by plucking the strings with the fingers, rather than by using the bow. Why is *pizzicato* never translated? Beats me. Perhaps just because *pizzicato* is a delightful-sounding word. It certainly sounds better than "plucked." Musicians sometimes shorten it to "pizz" (pronounced "pitz"), when they're discussing a passage, as in, "Oh, I forgot, those three notes are pizz," but I don't think I've ever heard a colleague say anything on the order of, "Those three notes are plucked."

Brass Quintet – Brass Magic

A "brass quintet" consists of two trumpets, French horn, trombone, and tuba. When I've attended performances by brass quintets, I've been struck by a big difference, a visual difference, between a brass quintet concert and, say, a string quartet concert. When we watch a string quartet, we see lots of movement—of arms, hands, fingers, instruments—and the movements correspond precisely to the notes we hear. But for those of us who don't play a brass instrument, watching brass players play almost seems like watching a magic show: the number of times the players move their fingers, or in the case of trombonists their slides, doesn't nearly add up to the number of notes we hear, and where the players put their fingers or slides doesn't seem to bear any relation to which notes they're playing. What's the reason behind these mysterious discrepancies? It's that most of what brass players do is done with the lips, and therefore invisible to us. The trumpet, horn, and tuba usually just have three or four keys, or valves, but even with just one key depressed the player can play a whole series of different notes just by varying lip shape and air pressure. Add up the various series, each series different, and the brass magicians have all the notes they need. It's also just with the lips and air pressure, invisibly, that brass players change volume and tone color. Abracadabra!

Frets

The guitar, the lute, and the viola da gamba all have frets. Have you ever wondered why? Well I can tell you this: it's not so that the players can find the notes. Think about it: violinists and violists do without frets, and even cellists and double bass players, whose strings are as long or longer than those of the guitar, find their notes just fine without frets. But the guitar, the lute, and the members of the viola da gamba family are much less powerful than the members of the modern violin family, and they need help to be heard. That's where the frets come in. If you press a string down with just your finger, your soft flesh absorbs vibrations and takes away some of the sound. But frets are made of hard material like bone, plastic, or even metal, and when you press a string on a fret, the fret doesn't absorb the vibrations— or hardly absorbs them—and that helps the fretted instrument sound louder than it otherwise would.

Harp

If you have a chance to attend an orchestra concert anytime soon and one of the pieces on the program calls for a harp, make sure to watch the harpist's feet. They'll be busy. The modern concert harp has forty seven strings, but it also has seven foot pedals, each of which controls one set of strings for each note of the scale. The A pedal, for example, controls all the A strings on the harp, and can change their length so that they sound A-natural or A-sharp or A-flat. As they play, harpists have to set and reset their pedals constantly, and quickly, to prepare for the notes that are coming up. Meanwhile, shifting your view from the feet to the hands, you may, if you're sharp, detect an interesting phenomenon: harpists don't use their pinkies. Since it's the weakest finger, and since on the harp it provides no reach advantage—the ring finger stretches farther—the pinkie is just along for the ride.

Percussion Instruments

In some ways, composers are like chefs: they're always looking for interesting or even exotic flavors. Or like painters, experimenting with compelling colors and color combinations. And percussion instruments, whether alone or in combination, have always been very useful ingredients for adding flavor and color to orchestral compositions. Contemporary composers have been especially enthusiastic in their use of percussion instruments, sometimes calling for whole stages full of instruments that are struck, scraped, or tinkled, along with instruments that only exist as computer programs and electronic circuits. But again, the basic idea isn't new. For centuries, for example, composers have used big drums to evoke the sounds of battles and storms, and by the end of the nineteenth century, concert audiences had already gotten to know the sounds of triangles, cymbals, chimes, gongs, xylophones, celestas, tambourines, and glass armonicas, not to mention crotales, anvils, and chains.

Drumsticks

Percussion players can vary the sounds of their instruments by using different kinds of drumsticks, or drumsticks with different kinds of heads. Timpani (kettle drum) players, for example, use sticks that range from very soft to very hard. The heads of "normal," or "regular" timpani sticks are made of felt—hard felt covered with soft felt—but the softest timpani stick heads are made of sponge, and the hardest are made of solid wood. Just imagine the difference in sound between a drum struck with sponge and a drum struck with wood. The sticks that xylophone, marimba, and glockenspiel players use are called mallets, and again, mallets with different heads produce different sounds. The glockenspiel, for example, consists of a set of steel bars. Striking those bars with a rubber-headed mallet is one thing, but striking steel with steel is quite another, and the sound can be penetrating, to put it mildly. When I was in graduate school, I played in the orchestra for a performance of Emmanuel Chabrier's opera *Le roi malgré lui*, and my seat in the pit was directly in front of not one but two glockenspiels being played with steel mallets. I'm still not sure I've recovered.

Orchestra Metals

Shall we take a brief metallurgical tour of the orchestra? There's a lot to see. The bars of glockenspiels and celestas, for example, are made of steel. So are some of the strings of stringed instruments, and almost all strings are wound with very fine wire made of steel, silver, or aluminum. The bodies of timpani are made of copper, and brass instruments are made of, well, brass, which is an alloy of copper and zinc. French horns, though, may also be made of nickel silver, an alloy of copper, zinc, and nickel, or nickel brass, an alloy of copper, tin, and nickel. In the flute section you may find flutes of gold, silver, platinum, or some combination of those metals, and back in the string section the players' bows may have gold or silver winding near the grip and gold or silver at the tip. We're back to steel for the screws, keys, and fittings on many of the instruments of the orchestra, and heaven knows what metals I've left out.

Wind Instruments

A wind instrument is any instrument whose sound is produced by a column of air vibrating inside some sort of tube, or pipe. But to clear up a common misconception: wind players don't actually try to blow large quantities of air into or through their instruments—the air inside a wind instrument is already there. Picture a flute, for example, or a tuba, or the pan pipes. The tubes or pipes are open, not closed, so the air is *always* there. What wind players use their breath for is to produce vibrations, and the vibrations that are produced, whether in a reed or in the air of a mouthpiece, are what cause the column of air inside the instrument to vibrate. Think, for example, about making a sound with an empty soda bottle: you're not blowing into it, you're blowing across the top, and the vibrations you set up that way are what makes the air inside the bottle vibrate. Well, that's exactly the way the flute works. Flutists don't blow into their mouthpieces, they blow across them. And tuba players don't have to fill a whole tuba with air, thank goodness, they just have to make a buzzing sound in their mouthpieces.

Which Came First?

So here's the famous riddle: Which came first, the chicken...or the violin? Or the piano? Or the valved horn? The members of the modern violin family had been perfected by the mid-to-late-1500s, and by 1600 the Baroque era in music had begun, with an explosion of music for the violin. The piano was invented in about 1700 and eventually mass produced, and by 1775 the Classical era in music was in full swing, with an explosion of music for the piano. The ranges and possibilities for brass instruments were increased enormously in the early 1800s when instrument makers figured out how to add valves to horns and trumpets, and the 19th century, the Romantic era in music, saw composers writing ever-more demanding and sophisticated music for the brass sections of their ever-expanding orchestras. Did all the new inventions fit new artistic trends, or were they responsible for them? Or both?

Glass Armonica

In May of 1761, Benjamin Franklin was in Cambridge, England, and he heard a man play a performance on musical glasses. They were crystal wine glasses filled with different levels of water, and when the performer rubbed the edges of the glasses, they produced different notes. Franklin was entranced by the sound, and he invented a mechanical version of the musical glasses that he called the glass armonica. Franklin's instrument consisted of a set of glass bowls mounted on a spindle in a water-filled trough. The player turned the spindle with a foot pedal, and rubbed the bowls with moistened fingers. The instrument became extremely popular for a while—Mozart even wrote a couple of pieces for it, and much later Saint-Saëns used it in his *Carnival of the Animals*. One famous and apparently highly-skilled player of the glass armonica was Franz Anton Mesmer, who used the instrument in group therapy sessions to help mesmerize his patients (see "Mesmer and Mozart," above).

ABOUT THE AUTHOR

MILES HOFFMAN is the founder and violist of the American Chamber Players, and the Virginia I. Norman Distinguished Visiting Professor of Chamber Music at the Schwob School of Music, in Columbus, Georgia. He has appeared as viola soloist with orchestras all across the United States, and his solo performances on YouTube have received well over 650,000 views. His radio modules, *A Minute with Miles*, are a daily feature of South Carolina Public Radio and other networks around the country. His musical commentary, "Coming to Terms," was broadcast weekly from 1989 to 2002 on NPR's *Performance Today*, and since 2002 he has been a classical music commentator for NPR's flagship news program, *Morning Edition*. He is the author of *The NPR Classical Music Companion: An Essential Guide for Enlightened Listening*, and he has written articles for *The New York Times, The Los Angeles Times, The Washington Post*, and *The Wilson Quarterly*. A distinguished teacher and clinician, and former dean of the Petrie School of Music at Converse College, he has presented countless master classes, workshops, children's programs, and other educational programs at schools, colleges, and conservatories around the country, and he has been a featured lecturer and keynote speaker for orchestras, chamber music series, festivals, and various professional organizations and conferences. He is a graduate of Yale University and the Juilliard School.